The Nature of the Will
in the Writings of Calvin and Arminius

The Nature of the Will
in the Writings of Calvin and Arminius

A Comparative Study

Alrick George Headley

WIPF & STOCK · Eugene, Oregon

THE NATURE OF THE WILL IN THE WRITINGS OF CALVIN AND ARMINIUS
A Comparative Study

Copyright © 2017 Alrick George Headley. All rights reserved. Except for brief quotations in critical publications or reviews, no part of this book may be reproduced in any manner without prior written permission from the publisher. Write: Permissions, Wipf and Stock Publishers, 199 W. 8th Ave., Suite 3, Eugene, OR 97401.

Wipf & Stock
An Imprint of Wipf and Stock Publishers
199 W. 8th Ave., Suite 3
Eugene, OR 97401

www.wipfandstock.com

PAPERBACK ISBN: 978-1-4982-3551-8
HARDCOVER ISBN: 978-1-4982-3553-2
EBOOK ISBN: 978-1-4982-3552-5

Manufactured in the U.S.A.   MAY 9, 2017

To Gwen
and our children, Garrit, Alaina, Andrew, and Amanda

Thus simply to will is the part of man, to will ill the part of corrupt nature, to will well the part of grace
—JOHN CALVIN, *INSTITUTES*, II.III.5

Free will is unable to begin or to perfect any true and spiritual good, without grace
—JAMES ARMINIUS, "HIPPOLYTUS," *WORKS*, 2:700

Contents

Preface | ix

Introduction | 1
Chapter 1   The Views of Free Choice in the Prelapsarian State | 21
Chapter 2   The Views of Free Choice in the Postlapsarian State | 39
Chapter 3   The Views of Free Choice in the Redeemed State | 73
Chapter 4   The Views of Free Choice in the Glorified State | 89
Conclusion | 96

Bibliography | 103

Preface

I BECAME INTERESTED IN the theological differences between John Calvin and James (Jacobus/Jacob) Arminius during my college years, in the first half of the 1990s. The Baptist church I grew up in faithfully proclaimed the unsearchable riches of Christ with vivid vibrancy. Though all the pastors of my youth had reputable divinity and theological degrees, I cannot recall any of them mentioning Calvin or Arminius, nor anything about Calvinism or Arminianism. These pastors, who were quite familiar with the differing viewpoints, did not feel the need to introduce that debate to their congregants. Their primary focus was on expositing the living and abiding word of God.

The first time I became aware of the great divide that exists between Calvin and Arminius and between Calvinism and Arminianism was during my first year at a Reformed college. When fellow students asked me what denomination I belonged to, I told them I was a Baptist. Naively, I had assumed being a Baptist was acceptable at a Christian college, since I considered myself to be a regenerate member of the body of Christ. However, I soon realized that being a Baptist at a Reformed college caused one to be viewed with some amount of suspicion. For, in response to my "I'm a Baptist" answer, I was told this means I am an Arminian. Having never heard this term, Arminian, I further inquired about the meaning of this appellation that was being ascribed to me. I was told that Baptists are Arminians who do not believe in the sovereignty of God. I was further told that, because I was a Baptist, and by extension an Arminian, I believed I had somehow saved myself by my own free will, as opposed to Calvinists, who believed that God is the one who saved them.

Preface

This was a lot for a non-theological yet Bible-believing and born again Christian to take in. Nevertheless, I immediately came to the conclusion that I must not be an Arminian, since I have always believed in the sovereignty of God and it had never occurred to me—not once—that I saved myself and that my salvation wasn't somehow the work of God. When I made a public profession of my faith and was asked by the elders, "Why are you coming now to be baptized and give your life to Christ?," I remember sitting before elders of my church and giving a very Calvinistic answer. In my own inarticulate manner, and with an answer that showed a lack of familiarity with the intricacies of theological matters, I told the elders that "God elects people and God saved me and it doesn't manner when I come; what matters is that I am coming now." The thought that I saved myself had never occurred to me until it was introduced to me by my Calvinists friends. As a result, in light of what I remembered saying in my profession of faith, I came to another conclusion: I must be a Calvinist; I just didn't know it.

The realization that I must not be an Arminian but an ignorant Calvinist did not put the matter to rest. Since the label Arminian, about which I had no knowledge, was being ascribed to me, I felt it my duty to investigate what Arminians actually believe. For, either my fellow (Reformed) students were ignorant of what Baptists believe, or they didn't truly understand what Arminius actually taught. Therefore, in order to satisfy my own lack of knowledge and clarify apparent misunderstandings, I began to read—hiding as I did—the writings of James Arminius in the college library. I hid because by this time I realized that to be labelled an Arminian at a Reformed college was, in the minds of many, tantamount to having a plague for which a cure was needed. Moreover, I hid because I did not want to perpetuate this (false) belief that I was an Arminian by being caught reading books by Arminius himself.

After a few weeks of reading, I got to the section at the end of one of the three volumes where Arminius often makes statements like, "That I never said," and repeatedly claims that many views being attributed to him are not his but flagrant misrepresentations. He at times refer to the mischaracterizations of his theological views as "falsities" and "slander." Though from a systematic and historical theological point of view, I did not then understand much of what I was reading, that Arminius was denying some of the theological deviations attributed to him was quite clear to me. Here was a man who felt he was misunderstood and was being misrepresented.

Preface

With my new knowledge, and armed with a few quotes, I began to ask students and some professors if they had ever read anything written by Arminius. To my surprise and dismay, all the students and all the professors I asked at the time had never read Arminius. My surprise was elevated to a measure of shock when I realized that those students who were the most vocal in their opposition to Arminianism had never read anything written by Arminius. I thought to myself that this posture of dogmatically commenting on Arminius and his theological beliefs without having read him is inconsistent with the love for truth and for neighbor that Christians ought to possess. I felt then that it was incumbent upon me to find out what Arminius actually believed and to sort out wherein lies the difference between his views and those of John Calvin. I had read enough during my college years to conclude that there is much that I didn't understand about this debate between the Calvinists and the Arminians; however, further study would have to wait.

During one of my years in seminary, I went into one of my professors's offices, as students sometimes do, and noticed that my Reformed professor had the three-volume set of Arminius's works tucked away at the bottom of his bookshelves. I thought to myself, "Wow! Here is someone I can dialogue with about Arminius and his theology." But I was again disappointed when I asked this professor, "Have you read those books by Arminius?" and he replied, "No, I have never read them, but I have heard that they are the most boring books you will ever read." After that experience, I stopped asking Reformed students and professors if they have ever read Arminius and I lost hope that I would ever meet someone of a Reformed and Calvinistic persuasion that has actually read Arminius.

Nevertheless, my interest in studying Arminius for the sake of the truth never abated. After graduating from one seminary, I had the opportunity to pursue another degree at another Reformed seminary. Here I encountered Dr. Richard Muller, who not only had read Arminius but had written a seminal work on the theology of Arminius. Being encouraged by this fact, I again began to read Arminius's writings. Throughout my college and initial seminary education, I was also reading Calvin's writings, particularly his sermons, and came to the conclusion that he too was often misrepresented by well-meaning Calvinists. I found that he was more of a pastor than the rigid systematic theologian he was often presented to be. Therefore, over the years I have come to enjoy reading the writings of both Calvin and Arminius and find them to be very stimulating. After much reading and reflection, I decided to share with a wider audience what I have learned over the years in the form of this little book.

The purpose of this book, then, is to compare Calvin's and Arminius's understandings of the will in the fourfold state of man[1]: the prelapsarian state, the postlapsarian state, the redeemed state, and the glorified state. I follow the fourfold model bequeathed to us by Augustine in his popular analysis of sin, with his *posse non peccare, non posse non peccare, posse peccare et non peccare,* and *non posse peccare.* In the introductory chapter, I explain the method of analysis used in this book and make relevant clarifications. Here I introduce the reader to the current state of scholarly literature and define major concepts and words used herein.

The second chapter commences, properly, the comparative part of the study by setting forth Calvin's and Arminius's views of free choice in the prelapsarian state of man. Here, I show that the differences that exist between the two theologians' understandings of man's will, as it relates to the constitution and function of the will in the state of innocence, set the stage for more evident differences that are present in the postlapsarian and redeemed states.

Since most of the literature deals with Calvin's and Arminius's views in this state, the third chapter, covering the postlapsarian state, is the longest. The differences between Calvin and Arminius become more evident in this state. Calvin defends the destruction of free choice in fallen man. Arminius, on the other hand, defends the preservation of man's freedom of choice in his fallen state.

The fourth chapter covers the redeemed state of man. The differences between Calvin and Arminius continue. Both theologians advocate freedom of choice in this state, but with differing understanding of what that freedom entails. For Calvin, the redeemed man necessarily perseveres in his faith, whereas, for Arminius, the redeemed man has the ability to reject the gospel and lose his salvation.

In the final chapter, on the glorified state, from the little written on the subject I make sound, logical inferences concerning the state of the will. For both Calvin and Arminius, the will finally experiences ultimate freedom of choice. I end with general conclusions relative to the entire work.

---

1. In this essay, the word "man" and its variations is often—but not entirely—used in the generic and inclusive sense to designate both man and woman. In some places, I have used words like "people" or "human being" and other similar words to accomplish the same goal of inclusivity.

Preface

This book is the product of a journey begun more than twenty-five years ago.[2] Along the way, I have received much help and encouragement. I am very grateful to those students whose judgements forced me to begin reading Arminius, to the elders of Zion United Reformed Church, who gave me a generous sabbatical to complete my thesis, to professors Dr. John Bolt, Dr. Lyle D. Bierma, and Dr. Richard A. Muller, my advisors at Calvin Theological Seminary, for their encouragement and guidance during my studies there, to Cheryl De Graaf, who proofread my thesis in 2004, to Dr. Winnie Klumpenhower, who proofread this manuscript for publication, and to Wipf and Stock Publishers for graciously granting me numerous extensions in my quest to complete this project. Though I have received encouragement and support from the above named individuals and entity, this in no way implies that they all agree with my arguments and conclusions. I have not in every case followed the suggestions of my advisors and proofreaders.[3] Therefore, any lingering errors in this work are solely mine.

---

2. This book is a modification and updating of my master's thesis, "The Nature of the Will" (2004).

3. Few are the occasions where this has occurred. Yet none of this was driven by rebellion; but as it was, I was motivated more by conviction..

Introduction

General Overview

IN THIS BOOK, I will compare and contrast the nature of the human will in the writings of John Calvin and James (Jacob) Arminius.

In light of recent critiques of comparative studies methodology expressed by scholars such as Richard Muller and Keith Stanglin, a brief defense of my approach is warranted at the outset. Stanglin's critique of the "dubious comparative methodology" used by numerous scholars of Arminius also applies to many scholars who labor in the field of Calvin studies.[1] The burden of Muller and Stanglin is not to argue that theologians from different eras should never be compared and contrasted. Rather, when such comparative studies are done, care must be taken to be sensitive to the historical and theological threads that have informed the thoughts of the thinkers being compared; they should not be torn away from their historical contexts in such comparisons.

At one level, it could be argued that the concerns about dubious comparative methodologies do not apply here, since Calvin and Arminius both appropriated the methods and categories of scholasticism in their theological discussions. However, some may argue that the concern still applies, since their theological contexts were somewhat different. Calvin, on the one hand, was a bridge theologian who stood between the earlier developments of Reformed theology and its later codification in the era of orthodoxy. Arminius, on the other hand, was a child, student, and theologian set right in the era of orthodoxy. Thus, one can argue that his program was different from that of Calvin. Hence, to compare them in the way I have

---

1. Muller, *Unaccommodated Calvin*, 7–8; Stanglin, *Assurance*, 4–5.

done would be illegitimate. However, that Arminius often (as we shall see later) names Calvin, a theologian from the Reformation era, and Beza, a theologian from the later period of codification and orthodoxy, as theologians whose ideas he is interacting and disagreeing with, pulls them into his theological context, making this particular comparison entirely legitimate.

In addition, it ought to be kept in mind that this is primarily a systematic theological study, not a historical one. Though I am aware of and have tried to be sensitive to the historical contexts of Calvin and Arminius, my goal is not merely to display them in their historical context regarding their views on the human will. Others have done adequate studies in this area. My goal is to look at the theological differences and similarities that exist between these two thinkers insofar as their views on the human will are concerned.[2] By focusing on the human will and the related doctrine of free will (choice), I am not thereby suggesting that the will and issues relating to it form the central organizing principle from which the rest of the theologies of Calvin and Arminius are deduced. There are other theological motifs—e.g., creation, sovereignty, knowledge of God, christology, assurance, justification, grace, God's justice-that hold a more dominant place in their thinking. Yet, despite not being a central motif and in spite of the concerns about comparative methodology, there is a place for this particular kind of study, especially since Arminius presents his view on free will as an alternative to that of Calvin. In addition, this study has contemporary relevance, since the theological stances of many Protestant churches today are evaluated and categorized largely on the basis of their level of deviation from or acceptance of the purported theological positions of Calvin and Arminius.

A theological study of the human will, according to Bernard McGinn, falls into two major divisions. One, the "abstract complex" approach, focuses on reconciling the contingent acts of human beings with divine predestination and foreknowledge. Questions such as, "How can it be said that human beings have a free will if God already knows what will happen in the future, either because he has predetermined what will happen or because he has exhaustive knowledge of all future events, including the actions of human beings?," are primarily discussed in this first approach.

The second approach to the study of the human will "is concrete and historical" and focuses on "the relation of man's freedom of choice in the

2. I am sympathetic to William den Boer's caution that constantly comparing Arminius [or Calvin for that matter] with his contemporaries in order to place him in his context may have the negative effect of implying that an author's "views are significant or interesting only when they depart from those of others" (*God's Twofold Love*, 42).

various states of history to sin and grace."[3] In explaining briefly the focus of this second approach, McGinn mentions that it is about "man's freedom of choice in the various states of history to sin and to grace." He then highlights the state of innocence before the fall, the state of sin after the fall, and the state of grace after redemption in Christ. He fails, however, to mention the final state of man in glory. I suspect he has good reasons for not including this final state of man. One reason is that he may not have considered that final state part of the "history" of man since no person alive has experienced that history of being in glory. He may also have limited himself deliberately since he was writing an introduction to a book that deals mainly with the first three states of man, addressing the final state only in a cursory manner.

Notwithstanding, in our analysis of the nature of the will in the writings of Calvin and Arminius, I will focus on the second division of the issue as presented by McGinn, and I will include a look at the glorified state. Therefore, in this study I will analyze Calvin's and Arminius's views of the will in light of man's fourfold state: the prelapsarian, the postlapsarian, the redeemed, and the glorified. This type of comparative study with explicit presentation of the fourfold state of man has, to my present knowledge, never been done insofar as it relates to Calvin and Arminius.[4]

When the human will is analyzed with due consideration to the fourfold state of man, it becomes clear that though there are some points of similarity between Calvin and Arminius,[5] there are points of significant differences in their understandings of the nature and function of the will in the original, fallen, redeemed, and glorified states of man. With respect to the first and the last states of human existence, though Calvin and Arminius are in general agreement concerning the function of the will, they take this basic position for very different reasons. In their views of man's will in the postlapsarian and redeemed states, the disagreement between Calvin and Arminius becomes much more evident.

---

3. McGinn, "Introduction," 7. McGinn also points out that Augustine is the master of the "concrete complex" approach, and Boethius the major influencer in the abstract complex approach, which deals with issues of providence, predestination, and contingency (p. 11).

4. I am aware of Thomas Boston's work that deals with the nature of man in the fourfold state and covers matters relating to the free will and choice of man (*Human Nature*, 1964). Nevertheless, it was not Boston's intent to compare Arminius and Calvin in that work.

5. For example, Richard Muller shows that Arminius used the tools of scholasticism handed down to him just as the other reformers; Muller, "Scholastic," 263–77.

In this book, all quotations and citations of Calvin's *Institutes* are from the Beveridge translation unless otherwise noted. Whenever I make corrections to translations based on the original languages, the original will always be cited and the correction made. However, not every citation from the original signals a correction to the translations.

Beginning with the second chapter, whenever I use the term "Arminian" or "Arminians," I am referring not to the various groups in history that have claimed or otherwise have had the term applied to them, but to the teachings of Arminius himself as understood from his writings.

Overview of the Writings of Arminius Used in This Book

Since the various writings of Arminius used in this book were originally composed as individual essays, speeches, and dialogues that were later compiled in a three-volume set—unlike much of the writings of Calvin, which are available in the separate works they were originally intended to be—I offer the following brief overview of the various writings and discourses of Arminius contained in *The Works of Arminius* translated by James Nichols that are referenced in this book.[6] In this brief overview, I am following the order of the writings as they appear in the *Works* and not in their chronological order.

The first relevant set of writings are three discourses of Arminius that were given "as introductory discourses to his divinity lectures, when he first occupied the Professor's Chair in the University of Leyden, at the close of the year 1603."[7] In *The Works of Arminius*, these three discourses appear under headings "Oration I," "Oration II," and "Oration III." The first oration deals with the issue of the object of theology. The second deals with the question of the author and end of theology. The third deals with the question of the certainty of sacred theology.[8]

Following the orations, the next major piece of writing bears the title "A Declaration of the Sentiments of Arminius."[9] After his conference with

---

6. Arminius, *Works*, 3 vols. For a chronological listing of all the works of Arminius, see Muller and Stanglin, "*Bibliographia Arminiana*."

7. Arminius, "Oration I," 1:321.

8. Note that there are two other orations dealing with the priesthood of Christ and addressing dissensions among Christians that were not used in this book.

9. Arminius, "Declaration," 1:580–732. For a modern translation, see Gunter, *Arminius and His Declaration*, 90–157.

INTRODUCTION

Gomarus in May of 1608, in response to the request of the High Court of the States of Holland for Arminius and Francis Gomarus, another professor at Leiden University, to submit their views in writing, Arminius asked that he might be permitted to present his views not only in writing but also verbally in person. The request of Arminius was granted, paving the way for him to declare his views and sentiments. This piece of writing presents a declaration of Arminius's sentiments on predestination, providence, freedom of the will, God's grace, the divinity of Christ, and justification before the Hall delegates of the States of Holland at The Hague on October 30, 1608. The "Sentiments" of Arminius, given the year prior to his death, is a mature and systematic presentation of his views on theological topics covered therein.

The next piece of writing is "The Apology or Defense of James Arminius."[10] Arminius wrote this "Apology" in response to certain defamatory articles that were being circulated. These thirty-one articles questioned Arminius's and Adrian Borrius's orthodoxy. Along with Borrius, a minister in Leiden, Arminius was viewed with suspicion and was accused of teaching novelty and heresy on certain points of doctrine. This "Apology" was written on October 10, 1608. Matters relating to justification by faith, the divine decree as it relates to necessity and contingency, God's grace, punishments for sin in this life, the extent of the atonement of Christ, the works of the unregenerate, etc. are addressed in the "Apology."

I have also made use of two pieces of writings referred to as "Disputations." The first of these is "The Public Disputations of James Arminius," which is also later entitled "Disputations on Some of the Principal Subjects of Christian Religion."[11] The title of the second is "The Private Disputations of James Arminius in the Principal Articles of the Christian Religion."[12] Carl Bangs informs us that Arminius, according to the academic expectations of the day, began writing and delivering disputations during 1604—a practice that continued until the time of Arminius's death in 1609. This activity resulted in twenty-four public disputations, published in 1609, and in seventy-nine private disputations, published in 1614. Bangs claims these disputations were to have been Arminius's definitive body of divinity. And though Arminius was unable to finish his disputations, they provide us with the most comprehensive systematic account of his views on a wide variety of theological topics. Bangs also points out that, in the English edition

10. Arminius, "Apology," 1:733–70; 2:1–63.
11. Arminius, "Public," 2:72–317.
12. Arminius, "Private," 2:318–469.

of Arminius's *Works* issued in 1825–1828, a twenty-fifth disputation on repentance was added to the public disputations.[13]

The next piece of writing by Arminius appears under the heading "A Dissertation on the True and Genuine Sense of the Seventh Chapter of St. Paul's Epistle to the Romans."[14] In the *Works*, the lengthy dedication is signed by "The nine orphan children of James Arminius of Oudewater" and dated "13th August, 1612."[15] Carl Bangs tells us that this dissertation was published in Latin in 1613 and that Arminius was in the process of revising the manuscript for publication during the last year of his life.[16] Arminius originally wrote this dissertation around the time when, as a minister in Amsterdam, he had a series of sermons on Romans 7 in which he went against the accepted Reformed view at the time and preached that Romans 7 deals not with a regenerate person but with a particular class of the unregenerate who is still under the law. Arminius's ministry in Amsterdam lasted from about 1587 to 1603. He began preaching on Romans 7 in 1591. Arminius's interpretation of Romans 7 became a source of theological difficulty for him, to the point that he was accused of Pelagianism. The difficulties that arose led Arminius to write this dissertation immediately after the series on Romans 7 was ended.[17]

Another of the writings used in this book is a letter composed by Arminius to Hippolytus a Collibus.[18] Hippolytus was an ambassador to the

---

13. Bangs, "Arminius and Reformed Theology," 142–43. For more recent discussions on the authenticity of the disputations, see Stanglin, *Missing Public*, 7–100; and Boer, *God's Twofold Love*, 23–34. Den Boer believes that there is sufficient uncertainty regarding the authorship of the disputations rendering them less suitable as original source material for the study of Arminius's theology. Den Boer, however, views them as indispensable secondary source material. Stanglin, on the other hand, has argued that the preponderance of the evidence is such that there should be no doubt that Arminius is the author of the disputations. As such, they should be viewed as primary source materials for the study of Arminius. Since, in a letter to Hippolytus a Collibus, Arminius himself references a public disputation (number eleven) as his own when he writes that "I have explained these my sentiments, with sufficient plainness, in the Thesis on Free Will which were publicly disputed in the University," and since all I have read on the matter of the human will in the disputations agree with what Arminius says elsewhere, I will proceed with the assumption that the disputations genuinely reflect the views of Arminius on the subject matter of this book (Arminius, "Hippolytus," 2:701).

14. Arminius, "Romans," 2:318–487.

15. Ibid, 2:487.

16. Bangs, *Arminius*, 186.

17. Bangs, "Arminius and Reformed Theology," 83.

18. Arminius, "Hippolytus," 2:689–705.

Dutch provinces from Prince Fredrick IV, Elector of the Palatine in Germany. The letter is dated April 5, 1608. Apparently, in an earlier meeting Fredrick had intimated to Arminius that there was talk in Heidelberg that he had heterodox views on some points of doctrine. Arminius gave a verbal response to Hippolytus, who in turn requested that Arminius commit the thoughts of his verbal response to written form. Therefore, in this letter, Arminius puts in written form, as Hippolytus had requested, his views on the divinity of the Son of God, providence, predestination, grace and free will, and justification. Arminius also expected that this letter to Hippolytus would serve to clear his name.

I have also referenced "Certain Articles to Be Diligently Examined and Weighed."[19] It appears that these articles are just that—articles. Carl Bangs tells us, "The articles appear to come from his Leiden years [1603–1609] because they deal with issues that arose within the Leiden faculty. One issue that arose at Leiden revolved around a controversy Arminius had with Trelcatius over the communication of the divine essence from Father to Son."[20] There are twenty-nine articles covering various points of doctrine and life.

I have made use of three documents in volume 3 of Arminius's *Works*. The first is entitled "Friendly Conference with Dr. Junius."[21] This is a written debate between Francis Junius and Arminius over the matter of predestination. Arminius and Junius agreed to engage in a confidential discussion by way of letters concerning issues of predestination. In this conference, Junius responds to twenty-seven propositions of Arminius. For every response of Junius, Arminius offers a counter response. This correspondence between Arminius and Junius took place in 1597.

The second document in volume 3 that has been useful for this study is entitled "Modest Examination of Dr. Perkins's Pamphlet."[22] William Perkins had published a pamphlet that dealt with the mode and order of predestination and the amplitude of divine grace. In this pamphlet, Perkins presents the supralapsarian predestinarian view of Beza. Arminius wrote a response to Perkins with the hope that Perkins would respond.[23] Perkins never saw Arminius's "Modest Examination," since Perkins died in 1602, just when Arminius was completing his answer to the pamphlet. Bangs

19. Arminius, "Certain Articles," 2:706–31.
20. Bangs, "Introduction," 1:xix.
21. Arminius, "Junius," 3:1–248.
22. Arminius, "Perkins's" 3:249–484.
23. Bangs, "Arminius and Reformed Theology," 107.

states that this examination of Perkins's pamphlet "is . . . the groundwork of Arminius' doctrine of grace."[24]

The third document used from volume 3 is entitled "Examination of the Theses of Dr. Francis Gomarus Respecting Predestination."[25] This examination was written in 1604–1605. After Francis Junius's death in October of 1602, Arminius was called upon to fill the vacancy as professor at the University of Leiden. Arminius's proposed appointment was met with opposition from a number of people, including Gomarus. Eventually, Arminius was appointed as professor of theology at Leiden. But not long after embarking upon his work at Leiden, Arminius was involved in a bitter controversy with Gomarus on the issue of predestination. As a result, Gomarus composed thirty-two theses on predestination. It is to these theses that Arminius responded.

In all these writings of Arminius, I see no significant change in his doctrine of the human will. There no evidence that Arminius once held to the "bondage of the will" view, as taught by Calvin and Beza, which he later abandons for his own novel view. He never held to nor taught the view of Calvin and Beza on the matter of the human will. What I have observed is development and clarification of thought, which Arminius was forced, by the theological climate and circumstances of the day, to articulate. As such, I find no movement in the thought of Arminius that suggests he at one point in his life held a view of the human will that he forsook at a later point and time in his life. Granted, some have held that Arminius did change from holding to Beza's strict (superlapsarian) predestinarian view to a softer (infralapsarian) view of predestination.[26] That he studied in Geneva under Beza, who recommended him highly, does not provide sufficient evidence to warrant the conclusion that Arminius had previously held to Beza's theory of predestination.[27] In his role as a student in Geneva, Arminius may have felt it was not his place and did not need to challenge the revered Beza regarding his views of free will and predestination. Arminius's silence on these theological issues during his time in Geneva is not to be taken as consent with respect to Beza's teaching. In addition, that Arminius, shortly after embarking upon

---

24. Ibid., 126.

25. Arminius, "Gomarus," 3:521–658.

26. Kendall, *Calvin and English*, 141; Boer, *God's Twofold Love*, 14.

27. For further discussion on this issue of a lack of transition in Arminius's thought, see Bangs, "Arminius and the Reformation," 159–64; Arminius, "Arminius and Reformed Theology," 1–12; Bangs, *Arminius*, 138–41; Stanglin, "Overview," 1–5.

his pastoral ministry in Amsterdam, failed to respond to and defend Beza's view of predestination against two ministers who departed from that view is no proof that Arminius only then "began to doubt the correctness of Beza's predestinarian viewpoint."[28] It is most likely the case that, as I have stated, Arminius never held to Beza's view and, when called upon to do so, could not, in good conscience, defend the stricter view of predestination.

A Survey of Discussions on Free Will in Calvin and Arminius

The debate about the nature of the will is one of the enduring discussions in the study and development of theology. William Cunningham is certainly not exaggerating when he says, "There is perhaps no subject which has occupied more of the time and attention of men of speculation."[29] Most are familiar with the debates between Augustine and Pelagius, Luther and Erasmus, and the more recent debates between Calvinists and Arminians over the nature and function of the will.[30] Popular sentiment sees Arminians as arch defenders of the doctrine of human free will in salvation. Calvinists, on the other hand, are seen as arch opponents of free will. Notwithstanding these popular sentiments, it is clear that there are discontinuities and even disjunctions between what Calvin taught and what Calvinists today teach and believe.[31] The same is true—even more so—of Arminius and Arminians.

Many early works touched on Calvin's view of the human will en route to addressing some other area of Calvin's thought or en route to taking a comprehensive look at his theology.[32] Dewey Hoitenga's claim that "critical examination of Calvin's account of the will is almost totally absent in the writings of Reformed theologians and Calvin scholars of the past" still holds true for today.[33]

---

28. Boer, *God's Twofold Love*, 14

29. Cunningham, *Historical Theology*, 1:569.

30. Augustine, *Anti-Pelagian Writings* (1992); Luther, *Bondage* (1976); Winter, trans., *Erasmus-Luther* (1961); Pinnock, "From Augustine to Arminius," 15–30; Boyd, *God of the Possible* (2000). Other useful summaries and expositions of the debates can be found in Witt, "Creation," 43–80. See also Sproul, *Willing to Believe*.

31. I would not go as far as Kendall does in seeing Beza and much of subsequent Calvinism as a major revision of Calvin's theology; Kendall, *Calvin and English*, 1–238.

32. Some works that fall into these categories are: Niesel, *Theology of Calvin* (1956); Kendall, *Calvin and English*, 1–238; Torrance, *Calvin's Doctrine of Man* (1957).

33. Hoitenga, *John Calvin*, 12.

However, as Hoitenga seeks to fill the gap in this area of Calvin studies, his analysis is deficient on a number of counts. According to Hoitenga, Calvin's view of the human will is inconsistent "first, in his account of the relationship of the will to the intellect as God created them and second, in his account of what happened to the will when it was corrupted in the fall."[34] Though Hoitenga faults Calvin for being illogical in his view of the pre-fall and post-fall states of the will, I will subsequently show that, given Calvin's biblical methodology, he is being quite logical. Richard Muller, in the foreword to Hoitenga's book, points out that there appears to be a "logical inconsistency" and incompleteness in Calvin's discussion of the will in the *Institutes*.[35]

In trying to set forth a proper understanding of Arminius, Witt agrees formally with both contentions of Hoitenga. Witt states that Calvin's focus on divine sovereignty led him radically to maintain a clear distinction between the Creator and the creature. In this way, God's absolute glory is maintained. In Witt's understanding of Calvin, though God as Creator is separate from his creation, he is very much involved in the governing and sustaining of all his creatures by means of providence. However, Witt's further assertion, that Calvin's view of providence leads to determinism, fails to do justice to the various nuances in Calvin's thought.[36] Interestingly, from a slightly different perspective, Charles Partee shows that Calvin's view of predestination, which would include providence, does not necessarily entail determinism.[37]

Anthony Lane assesses Calvin's view of the will slightly differently. Lane affirms, in answer to the question, "Did Calvin believe in freewill?," that not even Calvin himself could give a clear answer. Lane claims, "At different stages in man's history different degrees of freedom are conceded to the will."[38] Thus, there were times when Calvin vehemently opposed free will and there were times when he argued for free will, depending on the state of man and depending on the views of his opponents. When responding to Albert Pighius, a Roman Catholic polemicist, Calvin mainly argues that man does not have free will post-fall. When arguing against the Libertines, Calvin

---

34. Ibid, 14.
35. Muller, "Foreword," 6, 9.
36. Witt, "Creation," 84, 85, 86, 89.
37. Partee, "Determinism," 123, 128.
38. Lane, "Did Calvin?," 86.

mainly argues that man does have free will. For Lane, then, the question "Did Calvin believe in freewill?" is too general. Here, I agree with Lane.

Susan Schreiner offers a similarly nuanced view when she argues that when Calvin is addressing the errors of Stoics, who were determinist, he treats the human will more positively, allowing for some freedom. However, when dealing with Epicureans, who believe in a more general providence of the deistic stripe, Calvin is more inimical to notions of human freedom.[39]

Muller picks up the discussion at the point of redemption subjectively experienced in faith.[40] Muller argues that at the moment of faith Calvin is neither a thoroughgoing philosophical voluntarist nor a thoroughgoing philosophical intellectualist. Nevertheless, Muller concludes that Calvin's voluntarist leaning is not thoroughgoing philosophical voluntarism but a "soteriological voluntarism."[41] A brief definition of a voluntarist would be someone who holds to the priority of the will over the intellect in issues of choice. Intellectualism prioritizes the intellect over the will.[42] Though the statements of Muller are indirectly applicable to Hoitenga, Muller is primarily responding to R. T. Kendall, who claims that later Calvinism does not stand in continuity with Calvin. On the matter of faith, Kendall holds that Calvin was an intellectualist whom later Calvinism made out to be a voluntarist.[43] In this way, Kendall makes Calvin appear to be more in agreement with Arminius.

Thus far, I have been focusing on Calvin. However, within the realm of Arminius studies, one also encounters contradictory and inconsistent appraisals of his theology in general and of his view of the human will in particular. As I have noted earlier, the disparity between Arminius and the Arminians is far greater than that between Calvin and the Calvinists. As Alan Sell maintains, "In important respects, Arminius was not an Arminian."[44] In some cases, the divergence from Arminius is striking. The open view of God advocated by ostensibly Arminian theologians, Boyd and Pinnock for example, appears to go well beyond the teachings of Arminius.[45] No

39. Schreiner, *Theater*, 19–34.

40. Muller, "*Fides* and *Cognitio*," 207–24.

41. Ibid., 223.

42. See next section below for a fuller definition of this and other pertinent terms.

43. Kendall, *Calvin and English*, 19. Kendall also makes this point in "Puritan Modification," 199–214.

44. Sell, *Great Debate*, 97.

45. Hicks, "Was Arminius an Open Theist?," 146.

doubt, these theologians and others may argue that their view is the logical outworking of the theological ideas espoused by Arminius. One doubts whether Arminius would have followed the logical outworking of his views this far. Albert Einstein, for example, in declaring that "God does not play dice with the universe," was unwilling to follow what appears then to have been the logical conclusion of his research in quantum mechanics that at minute levels the universe is fundamentally unpredictable and disordered. Biblical consideration should restrain mere human logic. Without fully addressing the issue of whether or not established Arminianism truly reflects the teaching of Arminius, John Sanders affirms that open theism is not a separate specie but part of the genus of established Arminianism.[46]

I see similar contentions with regard to the teachings of the Remonstrants. John Mark Hicks, F. Stuart Clarke, and Carl Bangs would respectively contend, however, that Remonstrants' teaching then and Arminianism now are not the logical outworking of Arminius's theology.[47] The Remonstrants were Dutch followers of Arminius who defended and promoted his views after his death. The Remonstrants deduced five main points from the teachings of Arminius which were subsequently presented and condemned at the Synod at Dordt in 1618. To the five points presented by the Remonstrants, the Synod countered with what is popularly known today as the five points of Calvinism, or the doctrines of grace, summarized in the acronym TULIP, which stands for Total depravity, Unconditional election, Limited atonement, Irresistible grace, and Perseverance of the saints.

Hicks continues and, after a survey of various views, concludes that there are three basic positions on the question of Arminius's relation to the Remonstrants and Philip van Limborch in particular. Some see Arminius's theology and that of the Remonstrants as "essentially the same." Others allow for "several major differences but maintain that there is a logical connection between them." The last group, with which Hicks sides, maintains that "There is a radical difference between the two systems."[48] Clark, who fits into Hicks's last grouping, argues that "The Remonstrance . . . gives a false impression of the position of Arminius himself, whose objection to Calvin was that his doctrine of predestination was just not sufficiently

---

46. Sanders, "'Open Theism,'" 69–102.
47. Hicks, "Theology of Grace" (1985); Clarke, " Understanding," 25–35; Bangs, "Arminius and the Reformation," 155–56.
48. Hicks, "Theology of Grace," 19.

Introduction

Christocentric."[49] Bangs, who also fits in the third group, simply concludes, "The Arminian movements, however, because of their diversity do not point clearly to Arminius himself."[50]

Richard Muller would disagree with Hicks, Clarke, and Bangs on this point insofar as the Remonstrants are concerned. As Muller says, partly contradicting Hicks, "It is to Phillip Limborch that history owes the seventeenth-century codification of Arminian or Remonstrant theology."[51] In another place Muller concludes,

> Thus, the intricacies of Arminius' God-language, particularly as they became the foundation of a distinctively Arminian or Remonstrant doctrine of God in the writings of Episcopius and Limborch, are crucial to the whole Arminian system understood as a theological and philosophical construction of reality.[52]

Considering his historical sensitivities, I take Muller's use of the term "Arminian" as reference to the specific teachings of Arminius himself. Therefore, from the quotations above, it appears that Muller falls into Hicks's second grouping of a logical connection between Arminius and the Remonstrants.

In the first group, consisting of those who see an essential similarity between the system of Arminius and that of the Remonstrants, we have Lambertus J. van Holk, writing in 1962, who maintains that "There is no vast difference between the Arminius who lived in the seventeenth century and the Arminianism that exists today," and Gerrit J. Hoenderdaal, who argues that the biblical, practical, and irenic spirit of "the theology of the Remonstrant Brotherhood . . . express the essence of his [Arminius'] theology."[53] Thus, both van Holk and Hoenderdaal would also disagree with the radical difference claim of Hicks et al.

The literature also contains contrary claims about Arminius's view on free will. The popular view that Arminius is the forefather of present-day Arminianism and, as such, a staunch advocate of free will is not without its challengers. Barry E. Bryant contends, "That Arminius advocated freewill

---

49. Clarke, "Understanding," 35.
50. Bangs, "Arminius and the Reformation," 155.
51. Muller, "Federal Motif," 115; see also ibid., 108, 116, 118–19, 121, 122.
52. Muller, *God, Creation*, 101.
53. Van Holk, "From Arminius to Arminianism," 27; Hoenderdaal, "Life and Struggle," 25.

is a well-documented fact of history."[54] Witt's entire dissertation proceeds with the assumption that Arminius believed in free will. On the other hand, Hicks categorically states, "Arminius does not believe that man in the fallen state possesses a free will" in the sense of being able to do and will any true good.[55] Robert Dell, however, holds that Arminius taught both bondage and freedom of the will.[56]

To complicate matters even more, there has been a general neglect of the study of Arminius and his original theology, either for fear of being considered crypto-Arminian on the part of Calvinists or because of general apathy on the part of Arminians.[57] Though there has been an effort in recent years to overcome this lack and though there has been "revival of interest in and study" of Arminius, much more work needs to be done before Arminius is taken off the list of neglected theologians.[58] There is widespread neglect in the study of Arminius's theology. Moreover, it appears that some of the few researchers who have written on Arminius and his theology do so with theological biases. While Bangs and Hoenderdaal make Arminius appear in continuity with the Reformed and Calvinistic tradition,[59] Witt makes him look quite like a thoroughgoing Catholic, and Pinnock makes him look like the true forefather of his brand of Arminianism. R. C. Sproul deals with Arminius in his book on the history of the controversy over free will only to pass him off as a synergistic anti-Calvinist.[60] Even as Eef Dekker has proven that Arminius's logical commitment had a deterministic impact on his theology, Witt contends, "it is not clear that Ramus had a significant effect on the content of Arminius' theology."[61] Petrus Ramus, a Huguenot,

54. Bryant, "Molina, Arminius," 96.
55. Hicks, "Theology of Grace," 36.
56. Dell, "Man's Freedom," 148.
57. Muller, *God, Creation*, 3; Cameron, "Arminius—Hero or Heretic?," 213. Stanglin, "Overview," 3; Stanglin and McCall, *Jacob Arminius*, 3–4. Since the completion of my master's thesis in 2004, a few more books and articles have been written about Arminius and his theology.
58. Stanglin, "*Bona Conscientia*," 361.
59. Hoenderdaal, "Life and Struggle," 25; For example, Hoenderdaal says, "Much of Calvinism can be found in the theology of Arminius; but he tried to be a Calvinist in a rather independent way." With regards to being Reformed, Muller's position is that Arminius was ecclesiastically, but not confessionally, Reformed, though there were numerous points of agreements between him and the Reformed churches and theologians in the Netherlands at the time; Muller, "Arminius and the Reformed Tradition," 40, 46–48.
60. Sproul, *Willing to Believe*, 125ff.
61. Dekker "Analysis of a Letter," 118–39; Witt, "Creation," 206; In addressing the

popularized a system of logic that was often used in theology. Ramist logic of bifurcations was viewed by some to be deterministic. In many Protestant church and seminary communities, the mention of the name Arminius invites acrimonious criticism and swift condemnation.

In addition to the differences among scholars in each camp, a few believe that, with further study and more understanding of the issues involved, some kind of rapprochement between Arminians and Calvinists is possible.[62] Certainly, my purpose in presenting these varying viewpoints on Arminius and Calvin is not to suggest that I am going to now resolve all the issues involved and bring unity out of disunity. My purpose is to survey the general scholarship comparing the nature of the will in Calvin and Arminius and to highlight that there is much more work to be done in addressing the relationship between Calvin's and Arminius's views on the freedom of the will.

Definition of Terms

In examining this difficult subject, it will be helpful to define some key terms used in the discussion. The first term that needs defining is the term "will." Vernon J. Bourke, whose work gives us a rather comprehensive treatment of the will, defines will in a variety of ways. For our purposes, it is useful to note that Bourke points to a tradition where will means intellectual preference, to another tradition that assumes will means rational appetite, and to yet another tradition that defines will in terms of freedom.[63] My interest is in the last mentioned tradition within which, in order to avoid equivocation, I will locate a more precise definition of will that stands within the Christian tradition.

The two primary words from which our English word "will" is derived are *voluntas* and *arbitrium*. *Voluntas* ordinarily means "the faculty of will resident by nature in all spiritual beings."[64] Will defined as *voluntas* must be distinguished from *arbitrium*, which ordinarily means "choice, decision,

---

matter of scholasticism as it relates to Calvin, Richard Muller maintains that the scholastic method as method "does influence content . . . but it does not determine the final result of an argument" (Muller, "Scholasticism in Calvin," 251).

62. Dell, "Man's Freedom," 214, 257; Craig, "Middle Knowledge," 141–64.
63. Bourke, *Will in Western*, 9–11.
64. Muller, *Dictionary*, 330.

[or] judgment."⁶⁵ In terms of a reference point within the Christian tradition, this distinction between *voluntas* and *arbitrium* goes back to Augustine and Aquinas⁶⁶ and has been accepted, though not always clearly articulated, by a preponderance of the theologians within the scholastic tradition, including Calvin and Arminius. *Voluntas* may be understood as the faculty of the will that has been given by God to all men. *Arbitrium*, on the other hand, refers to the function of the faculty of will. *Voluntas*, then, is the apparatus and *arbitrium* is the activity or use of the apparatus. Thinking of the difference between having legs and walking may help to illuminate the distinction I am making.⁶⁷

With the definition of the term will in place, I turn secondly to define the concept of "free will." What does "free" mean in the term "free will?"⁶⁸ The word in the Latin is *liberum*. It generally means liberty or freedom from compulsion. When we say that man possesses or does not possess free will, do we have in mind free *voluntas* or free *arbitrium*? What is often meant is free choice.

John Feinberg, a compatibilist, defines free choice as "the use of one's faculties to make choices between any given alternatives without any external or internal hindrances," and he defines freedom as the power to choose good or evil.⁶⁹ Compatibilists believe that free will (choice) and determinism are not mutually exclusive concepts that cannot be harmonized. Incompatibilists, on the other hand, usually hold that the one concept necessarily excludes the other. If there is free will (choice), the incompatibilist will argue, there cannot be determinism.

After tracing different definitions of free will given by the philosophers and the ecclesiastical writers, in the *Institutes*,⁷⁰ Calvin takes various elements from the philosophers and ecclesiastical writers while rejecting others and concludes, "We now perceive in what it is they suppose the faculty of

---

65. Ibid., 43, 330; Muller also argues for a distinction between *voluntas* and *arbitrium* in Muller, "Gambit," 272.

66. Alexander, *Theories of the Will*, 105, 137; For other useful discussion on the will similar to that of Alexander's see Arendt, *Life of the Mind: Willing* (1978).

67. Forlines, *Classical Arminianism*, 6–7. Here, Forlines speaks of a difference between personhood (constitution) and personality (function) in order to explain the same distinction I am making here.

68. In addition to the works of Alexander and Arendt, see the following for a discussion of free will: Gilson, *Spirit of Medieval Philosophy*, 304–23.

69. Feinberg, "Doctrine of Human Freedom," 10.

70. Calvin, *Institutes*, II.ii.2–4, 8.

INTRODUCTION

free choice [*liberi arbitrii*] to consist—viz. in reason and will [*voluntate*]."[71] Further in his exposition, Calvin arrives at his understanding of free will when he says, "In this way, then, man is said to have free choice [*Liberi . . . arbitrii*], not because he has a free choice [*liberam . . . electionem*] of good and evil, but because he acts badly voluntarily and not by compulsion."[72] This is perhaps the most direct definition of free will that we have from Calvin.

In other places, however, when discussing free will, it seems Calvin—for the sake of the debate—assumes his opponents' definitions of free will. For example, in response to the Council of Trent, Calvin says, "Let us not raise a quarrel about a word. But as by free choice [*liberum arbitrium*] they understand a faculty of choice [*eligendi*] perfectly free [*libera*] and unbiased to either side."[73] Notice that in this definition Calvin is giving and accepting another's definition of free will for the purposes of argument. When responding to Pighius, Calvin accepts that "People generally understand a free will [*liberam voluntatem*] to be one which has it in its power to choose [*eligere*] good or evil, and Pighius also defines it in this way."[74]

Generally, Arminius's definition of free will is similar and at the same time different from that of Calvin. In his "Public Disputations," article XI.I, he says, "The word, *arbitrium*, 'Choice,' or 'Free Will,' properly signifies both the faculty of the mind or understanding, by which the mind is enabled to judge about anything proposed to it,—and the judgment which the mind forms according to that faculty."[75] Here, Arminius combines both the faculty and the

---

71. Ibid., II.ii.4; *Calvini, Opera Omnia*, 2:190.

72. Calvin, *Institutes*, II.ii.7; *Calvini, Opera Omnia*, 2:191: "*Liberi ergo arbitrii hoc modo dicetur homo, non quia liberam habeas boni aeque ac mali electionem, sed quia male voluntate agit, non coactione.*" Note that the Beveridge translation fails to translate "*male.*" This definition comports with what Hoitenga considers to be a minimalist definition of free will, as opposed to a maximalist definition, which would include the free choice (freedom of indifference or freedom of contrary choice)—denied by Calvin—to do good and evil; Hoitenga, *John Calvin and the Will*, 30.

73. Calvin, *Selected Works*, 148; *Calvini, Opera Omnia*, 7:474: "*De verbo ne moveamus rixam. Sed quia per liberum arbitrium intelligent eligendi facultatem, quae sit in utramque partem libera et soluta.*"

74. Calvin, *Bondage*, 69; *Calvini, Opera Omnia*, 6:280.

75. Arminius, "Public," idem, *Opera Theologica*, 210: "*Arbitrii vox proprie significant mentis suie intellectus, tum facultatem, qua mens de aliqua resibi proposita iudicare potest: tum ipsum iudicium a mente secundum istam facultatem peractum.*" Note that the original is *arbitrii*, not *arbitrium*, and that the words "choice" and "free will" are supplied by the translator.

function in his definition of *arbitrium*, something Calvin does not do, except when assuming the definition of others for the sake of argument.

Another helpful statement of a definition of free will is provided by Thomas Aquinas. Wherefore, since liberty properly belongs to the will, Aquinas says, the most agreeable definition is to call free will an elective power that combines intelligence and appetite but inclines more to appetite.[76] John Gerstner, a later twentieth century theologian, defines free will simply as, "That by which man chooses whatever God causes him by God's presence or absence to choose."[77]

Now, though there was some minimal fluidity of use with the terms *voluntas* and *arbitrium*, and though it has been suggested that *arbitrium* and *voluntas* were used interchangeably, in these past discussions and as we will see later, it does not appear from my research that Calvin and Arminius always used these words interchangeably. It does appear, however, that Arminius, because of his identification of choice (*arbitrium*) as a necessary component of the will (*voluntas*)—as we will see later—uses the terms interchangeably on some occasions. This is reasonable since, for Arminius, there was no separation between the function and the faculty of the will. But even he did not always use the terms interchangeably.

Though at times other terms such as *eligere* and *electionem* are introduced, for the purpose of our discussion, I will consider *liberum arbitrium* to be the main term for free will, i.e., free choice. I also note that Muller, in his *Dictionary*, when defining free will points out that "*liberum arbitrium*" is "often loosely and incorrectly rendered 'free will.'"[78] Moreover, in his introduction to Bernard of Clairvaux's work, McGinn says, "it is the term 'free choice' (*liberum arbitrium*) and not "free will" (*libera voluntas*) which is the operative one in Bernard [of Clairvaux]."[79] Furthermore, citing Bourke and Etienne Gilson, McGinn advocates for a more precise distinction in our understanding of *voluntas* and *arbitrium* by appealing to Augustine when he says, "Augustine equated the will with the exercise of free choice and provided much impetus for that tradition which discusses grace and freedom primarily under the rubric of *liberum arbirium* rather than *voluntas*."[80]

---

76. Calvin, *Institutes*, II.ii.4; Calvin is correct in his assessment of Aquinas here; see Aquinas, *Basic Writings*, 790 (I.83.3).
77. Gerstner, "Augustine," 2:281.
78. Muller, *Dictionary*, 176.
79. McGinn, "Introduction," 8.
80. Ibid, 9.

Hence, in light of this tradition and in an effort to be more precise, rather than use the term "free will" in reference to *liberum arbitrium*, I will use the term "free choice." When I use the term "free will," unless otherwise noted or obvious from the context, I am referring to the freedom from coercion that is part of the nature of the faculty of will (*voluntas*). However, when quoting other authors who use the language of "free will," unless it is made clear through explicit statements or from the context that they are referring to freedom from coercion in relation to the faculty of will, I will assume that what they really are referring to is "free choice."[81]

Two other words in need of defining are "voluntarism" and "intellectualism." Voluntarism is the functional priority of the will over the intellect.[82] Intellectualism, then, would be the functional priority of the intellect (mind) over the will (heart). Another way of looking at the difference is to look at which faculty influences the other. If the will were the faculty that primarily influences the intellect, then this would be the voluntarist position, and vice versa.[83]

The ideas of voluntarism and intellectualism are born out of the medieval faculty psychology of the soul that goes all the way back to Aristotle. This psychology considers the soul of man to be divided into two main parts, intellect and will, with intellect having to do with the mind and will having to do with the affections/desire.[84] Though, traditionally, mind is often viewed as primarily the rational part of the soul, there is a voluntarist perspective that attributes rational function to the will.[85] The rationality of the will is seen in the choices that it makes. Another way of stating this is to say that the will has its own mind/intellect. For our purposes, I will assume that the will as *arbitrium* functions rationally. As I use the terms intellectu-

---

81. Other definitions of free choice can be found in Asselt, Bac, and Velde, eds., *Reformed Thought on Freedom* (2010).

82. Taylor, *Encyclopedia of Philosophy*, 270–72; see also Muller, "*Fides* and *Cognitio*," 211.

83. See Hoitenga, *John Calvin*, 24. The question of which faculty is nobler is not part of our discussion.

84. Bonansea, "Duns Scotus Voluntarism," 85. By way of history of the terms, Bonansea says in a footnote, "Although the term 'voluntarism' is of recent coinage, it has been used by historians to designate Scotus' philosophy and distinguish it from the intellectualism of St. Thomas Aquinas. The term was used for the first time by Ferdinand Tönnis in his article, 'Studien zur Entwickelungsgeschichte des Spinoza,' *Vierteljahrschrift für wissenschaftliche Philosophie*, 7 (1883), 169" (Bonansea, 83); see Wolter, trans., *Duns Scotus on the Will*, 31; Muller, *God, Creation*, 143.

85. Bourke, *Will in Western*, 55–71; Witt, "Creation," 419–21.

alism and voluntarism, I will keep in mind Muller's cautionary word that the terms "do not refer to excessive ratiocination in theology on the one hand and to an emphasis on freedom of choice on the other."[86] Nevertheless, determining whether Calvin and Arminius land on the intellectualist or the voluntarist side of the divide helps to illuminate their understandings of the human will in the fourfold state of human existence.

---

86. Muller, "*Fides* and *Cognitio*," 211.

Chapter 1

The Views of Free Choice in the Prelapsarian State

Calvin: Man's Choice Is Free within Bounds

HAVING DEFINED THE MAJOR terms, let us now proceed to an examination of Calvin's view of the nature of the will in its prelapsarian state. Based on my research, most authors believe Calvin teaches that human beings possess free choice in the prelapsarian state. This means human beings have the ability to make free choices that occur within the context of God's divine decrees. For Calvin, human beings, in the state of innocence, have the ability to freely choose the good and worship and serve God. This freedom of choice, however, also gives the first man and woman the ability to choose to do evil. One of the points of contention that arises here, however, is the charge that Calvin's free-choice view of man's will in the fallen state is inconsistent with his subsequent teachings. Arminius himself brings such charges against Calvin when he says, "But according to the opinion of Calvin and Beza God is made to be necessarily the author of sin."[1] This is so because in Calvin's understanding the freedom of choice possessed by the first parents was always and could only be used to fulfill what God had already decreed. Arminius is well aware that Calvin denies that God is the author of sin. However, Arminius believes that the charge is unavoidable in light of Calvin's understanding of God's ordination of the fall.[2] He cites Calvin and makes a case against Calvin's position, saying, "Adam did not fall necessarily, either with respect to a decree, appointment, desertion, or

---

1. Arminius, "Junius," 3:75.
2. Ibid, 3:76, 77.

permission."[3] Thus, for Arminius, the fall of Adam lies outside of God's "direct divine willing."[4] In Arminius's understanding, since the creature cannot but do what God decrees, it would be unjust for God to have directly willed the fall that would result in the condemnation of his creature.

Accordingly, Witt claims, incorrectly I believe, that "Calvin's insistence that Adam could have refrained from sin if he so willed [with the use of his free choice] conflicts with Calvin's equally strong insistence that God controls even the thoughts and wills of human beings."[5] In Witt's understanding, the charge that God is the author of sin is unavoidable in view of Calvin's teaching that God completely controls the thoughts and wills of human beings.[6] Witt wrongly faults Calvin for failing to understand the relation between God and the creation. As Witt states it, "Calvin's theology is marked by a profound ambivalence.... The chief source of Calvin's difficulty seems to have been an inability correctly to express the distinction between God and the world."[7]

Conversely, Susan Schreiner believes that Calvin expresses the distinction between God and the world in a right and appropriate manner. As the title of her book suggests, according to Schreiner, the creation for Calvin functions as the stage upon which God displays his glory. In creation, God daily places "himself in our view, that we cannot open our eyes without being compelled to behold him."[8] Laytham, complementing Schreiner's position, emphasizes the revelatory aspects of the creation, which function to render man inexcusable before God, thus vindicating God's justice in condemnation of the wicked. Schreiner's and Laytham's perspective is confirmed by Calvin's claim that "on each of his [God's] works his glory is engraven in characters so bright, so distinct, and so illustrious, that none, however dull and illiterate, can plead ignorance as their excuse."[9] And though they take differing paths to solve the issue, Calvin, like Arminius as we shall see, is concerned about deflecting the charge that God is the

---

3. Arminius, "Certain Articles," 2:716; Naturally, this use of "permission" is different from Arminius's own view of permission which allows for genuine contingency.

4. Muller, "God, Predestination," 442–43.

5. Witt, "Creation," 98; Witt cites Calvin's *Institutes*, I.xvi.8.

6. Witt, "Creation," 99–101, 384–87.

7. Ibid., 120, 121.

8. Schreiner, *Theater*, 5; Calvin, *Institutes*, I.v.1.

9. D. Laytham, "Natural Theology," 34–35; Calvin, *Institutes*, I.v.1, I.xv.1.

The Views of Free Choice in the Prelapsarian State

author of sin and about vindicating God's justice in the condemnation of the wicked.[10]

When he talks about the relation between God and man, the creature, Calvin uses language that underscores a *relationship*. In his comments on Genesis 1:26, Calvin speaks of man as one who *represents* the image of God. As God's representative, then, human beings image God by acting "as God's vicegerent in the government of the world."[11] However, this governing aspect of the image is a small part of the *imago Dei* in human beings. The greater part of the *imago Dei* is deduced from that which is restored and renovated in us in Christ. Thus, based upon passages such as Colossians 3:10, 19 and Ephesians 4:24, true knowledge, righteousness, and holiness—attributes that represent a significant part of the whole image—are the primary constitutive parts of the *imago Dei* in man.[12] These attributes, located with the intellect and will, reflect the glory of God as part of their image-bearing.

Thus, for Calvin, the intellect and the will as mere faculties, devoid of their proper function, are not properly to be considered the image of God. The *imago Dei* is *seated* primarily *in* the soul with its faculties of intellect and will. However, in a much broader sense, the *imago Dei* extends beyond the soul.[13] Though not material substances in terms of their position with respect to the *imago Dei*, the intellect and will are more *like* organs of the body upon or in which the image is engraven. For example, Calvin says, "As man was undoubtedly created to meditate on the heavenly life, so it is certain that the knowledge of it was engraven on the soul."[14] Commenting on Genesis 2:7, Calvin states "that *on this soul* God engraved his own image."[15]

The language of "engraven" and "engraved" connotes separation between God and his creatures that bear his image. We encountered similar language earlier when Calvin says, "on each of his [God's] works his glory

---

10. Calvin, *Institutes*, I.xv.1,8; Arminius, "Apology," 1:762; idem, "Junius," 3:44, 76–77; idem, "Perkins's," 3:342.

11. Calvin, *Genesis*, 1:94.

12. Ibid., 1:94–95; Calvin, *Institutes*, I.xv.4.

13. Calvin, *Institutes*, I.xv.3. Here, after stating that man is called the image of God with respect to the soul, Calvin explains further, saying, "though I retain the principle which I lately laid down, that the image of God extends to everything in which the nature of man surpasses that of all other species of animals"; see ibid., I.xv.7. The narrower sense of the image refers to the image as it is located in the soul.

14. Ibid., I.xv.6.

15. Calvin, *Genesis*, 1:112 (emphasis added); see ibid., 295–96, on Genesis 9:6.

is engraven in characters so bright, so distinct, and so illustrious, that none . . . can plead ignorance."[16]

In addition to the functions of creation noted above, as Calvin is poised to address specific issues relating to the will of man, he tells us that the reason he is including teaching about man's prelapsarian state is so that man may have a thorough knowledge of himself in order that he can know God properly. This proper knowledge of man includes knowledge of what he was originally created to be and knowledge of what he has become after Adam's fall. One reason Calvin starts with man's original state is to deflect blame from God for ills in man's nature that are not reflective of his original created state.[17] Since man was created perfect with free choice and since God continues to display his glory in creation, these tokens of divine graciousness are sufficient to remove the charge that God is the author of sin (Jas 1:13–14).

In developing this idea, Calvin argues that man in the prelapsarian state had genuine free choice. Man's soul, during his original state, is "formed to rectitude" in every part.[18] There is nothing in man's nature that compelled man to sin and fall. "Adam . . . might have stood if he willed, since it was only by his own will that he fell."[19] Had Adam willed to do the good, he could have stood if he would. He could because "There was soundness of mind and freedom of will to choose [*voluntas . . . eligendum libera*] the good."[20] However, the choice, ultimately considered, involves more than mere morality. Man, "In this upright state . . . possessed freedom of choice [*libero arbitrio*], by which, if he willed [*vellet*], he was able to obtain eternal life."[21] God made man with the ability to choose between good and evil with respect to earthly *and* heavenly matters. Thus, man was able to freely choose to continue to believe, trust, obey, and worship God.

In addition, Calvin acknowledges that the good gift of free choice with which man is endowed results from grace. For example, in his response to

---

16. Calvin, *Institutes*, I.v.1.

17. Ibid., I.xv.1, II.i.1; Calvin, *Bondage*, 40, 71.

18. Calvin, *Institutes*, I.xv.8.

19. Ibid, I.xv.8; idem, *Opera Omnia*, 2:143: "*Potuit igitur Adam stare si vellet, quando non nisi propria voluntate cecidit.*"

20. Calvin, *Institutes*, I.xv.8; idem, *Opera Omnia*, 2:143: ". . . *constabat mentis sanitas, et voluntas ad bonum eligendum libera.*" Though the word Calvin uses for choose is *eligendum* and not *arbitrium*, the idea is the same. *Eligere* is a verb that means elect, choose, select, or pick out (Stelten, *Dictionary*, 85).

21. Calvin, *Institutes*, I.xv.8; *Calvini, Opera Omnia*, 2:143: "*In hac integritate libero arbitrio pollebat homo, quo, si vellet, adipisci passet aeternam vitam.*"

the Council of Trent, Calvin rebukes the Scholastics for *not* making a "distinction between the grace of regeneration, which now comes to the succor of our wretchedness, and *the first grace* which had been given to Adam."[22] However, the first grace is different from the later effectual and saving grace of God. Though first grace blesses man with free choice to be able to choose to do good or evil, it does not *make* him choose and do good. However, as created in a state of original righteousness, man was more inclined to do good than to do evil.

Since man was created in such a state, without inclination but with the possibility of sinning (or remaining in a state of uprightness), why did he sin? This is a question that, according to Gerstner, "defies explanation."[23] Notwithstanding Gerstner's remarks, Calvin writes, "Adam . . . might have stood if he willed . . . ; but it was because his will [*voluntas*] was *pliable in either direction*, and *he had not received constancy to preserve*, that he so easily fell."[24] Thus, for Calvin, it is not simply because Adam misuses his free will and choice that he falls into sin. There is something withheld from man that allows for his infidelity and pride to cause the fall.[25] He lacks constancy—a gift that God chooses to withhold in the state of innocence. He is not given the gift of perseverance—a gift that Calvin later applies to the redeemed saints of God.

Though he teaches that man's bad use of his free choice is to blame for sin and the fall, Calvin also affirms that the will and decree of God, in some sense, also bring about the fall. Calvin writes, "God not only foresaw the fall of the first man, and in him the ruin of his posterity; but also at his own pleasure arranged it."[26] However, the blame for authoring sin does not land in God's lap.[27] God is not the author of sin. Though God superintends the fall, the immediate cause of the fall is man's misuse of his free choice. In this sense, man is the author of sin and the first sinner.

By locating the cause of the fall in the will and choice of man, Calvin shifts from intellectualism to voluntarism.[28] Notwithstanding this shift,

---

22. Calvin, *Selected Works*, 111 (emphasis added); Calvin, *Institutes*, I.xv.5; Arminius, "Junius," 3:110, 117.

23. Gerstner, "Augustine," 281.

24. Calvin, *Institutes*, I.xv.8 (emphasis added); idem, *Opera Omnia*, 2:143.

25. Calvin, *Institutes*, II.i.4.

26. Ibid., III.xxiii.7.

27. Ibid., III.xxiii.4.

28. Hoitenga, *John Calvin*, 45.

Calvin holds to a primarily intellectualist view of man in the created state of innocence. Calvin's prelapsarian intellectualism becomes evident in view of the roles he assigns to the intellect and will. Calvin states that the office of the intellect is "to distinguish between objects, according as they seem deserving of being approved or disapproved; and the office of the will, to choose and follow what the intellect declares to be good, to reject and shun what it declares to be bad."[29] Calvin clearly considers the intellect to be the faculty that has priority.

Calvin confirms the priority and dominance of the intellect when he further asserts, "For we do not deny that man was created with free choice, endowed as he was with sound intelligence of mind and uprightness of will."[30] However, "Let it be enough to know that the intellect is to us, as it were, the guide and ruler of the soul; that the will always follows its beck, and waits for its decision, in matters of desire."[31] Though the will clearly has a subordinate function, these expressions are not to be understood as implying that reason rules the will in such a way that it necessarily does what reason suggests as the good and the true.[32] This would destroy the concept of free will and choice and the will's office to choose whether to follow what reason suggests. As I mentioned above, it is appropriate when defining free will to understand that a measure of rationality must be ascribed to the will. Therefore, when the will exercises its choice and follows to good judgments of the intellect, it is acting rationally and freely.

Arminius: Man's Choice Is Free without Bounds

I now turn to examine Arminius's view of the human will in the prelapsarian state. As I do so, keep in mind that Arminius had the opportunity of

---

29. Calvin, *Institutes*, I.xv.7.

30. Calvin, *Bondage*, 47; Calvini, *Opera Omnia*, 6:263: "*Neque enim negamus, liberi arbitrii conditum fuisse hominem, qui et sana mentis intelligentia, et rectitudine voluntatis praeditus fuerit.*"

31. Calvin, *Institutes*, I.xv.7; see ibid., I.xv.2, 3, 8. Lane contends that "'always follows its beck' is too strong a translation;" and that, "the Latin implies only that the will is mindful of (*respicere*) reason" (Lane, "Did Calvin?," 86 n. 9) The McNeill/Battles edition of the *Institutes* translates the passage as "let it be enough for us that the understanding is, as it were, the leader and governor of the soul; and that the will is always mindful of the bidding of the understanding" (Calvin, *Institutes*, I.xv.7, Battles, trans., vol. 1).

32. Lane, "Did Calvin?," 73.

reading Calvin, and reading him well. Whatever critique he offers of Calvin's views ought to be viewed as sincere and reasoned.

In fact, the commonly held view is that Arminius regarded Calvin highly. Support for this view comes from Arminius's own statement that he valued Calvin's commentaries and recommended them highly to his students, though he was less enthusiastic in his recommendation of Calvin's *Institutes*.[33] To assure us that Arminius did value Calvin highly, Clarke tells us, "None of his [Arminius's] works were directed specifically against Calvin."[34] And as we have seen, a number of writers—Bangs, Hoenderdaal, Clarke, Cameron, and Hicks—would have us believe that, except for a few insignificant points, there is substantially no difference between the thought of Arminius and Calvin.

But as we consider Arminius's understanding of man's will in its prelapsarian state, we will see that, though there is a similarity in the resulting conclusion that man has free choice, there are significant underlying differences between Calvin and Arminius that pertain to God's activity in endowing man with free choice and to the location of free choice in man. Central to understanding Arminius's view of the nature of the will, not only in the prelapsarian state but in all the states of man, is comprehending Arminius's view of God, creation, and the relation that exists between God and his creation.

Though arriving at different conclusions, Muller and Witt both show that it is almost futile to try to understand Arminius's view of the human will without first understanding his view of the relation between God and the creation. Though he has subsequently modified his view on the centrality of the doctrine of creation in Arminius's theology, Muller captures the significance of creation in Arminius's system when he summarizes that, "If the Reformed system can be called without excessive reductionism and distortion, a theology of grace, the Arminian system may, perhaps, be called a theology of creation."[35] If this is true, note then that the difference between Calvin and Arminius on the nature and function of man's will and choice in salvation is not primarily a soteriological issue; the heart of the matter has to do with both theologians' understandings of the nature of God and his

33. Brandt, *Life of James Arminius*, 299–301; Bangs, "Arminius and the Reformation," 163–64; Clarke, "Understanding," 29; Muller, "Scholastic," 265.

34. Clarke, "Understanding," 26. Given that Arminius frequently names Calvin (along with Beza) as he argues against some of Calvin's ideas, Clarke is not entirely correct on this point; see Arminius, "Junius," 3:74–77, 214.

35. Muller, *God, Creation*, 268; see Muller, "God, Predestination," 445, 439, 440.

creation and the relationship that obtains between the two. On this point, in Witt's opinion, Arminius prevailed, where Calvin and his followers failed to understand the relation between God and creation by holding a view of God's sovereignty that tends in the direction of "cosmic determinism" that would "make God the efficient cause of evil in the world."[36]

What then is Arminius's view on God and creation and their relation? Arminius teaches both that God is the author and object of legal theology and that God and "his Christ" are the author and object of evangelical theology.[37] Legal theology addresses theology—reflection and reasoning about God and his relation to the world—prior to the fall of man as it relates to God's covenant with nature as created.[38] Arminius designates legal theology as a natural theology. Evangelical theology, then, addresses theology post-lapse; this is supernatural theology.[39]

The end (goal) of theology is union with God in legal theology and union with God *and Christ* in evangelical (Christian) theology. Here, in this state of innocence, we are concerned with legal theology.[40] As Arminius puts it, "The end of theology may with the utmost propriety be called, the union of God with man."[41] Arminius argues that this union of man with God is not an essential union where man is absorbed into God, nor is it a formal union where God's Spirit unites with man and enlivens him. Rather, the union between God and man is an objective and immediate union whereby God through his "faculties and actions . . . gives such convincing proofs of himself to man, that God may be said to be 'all in all'" and whereby "God unites himself to the understanding and the will of his creature, by means of himself alone."[42] The goal then of all human existence is union with God.[43] This goal of union with God is the goal of creation prior to and apart from the fall. In the creation of humans, then, God began

---

36. Witt, "Creation," 120, 121.

37. Arminius, "Oration I," 1:324–25, 336, 352, 354; Muller, *God, Creation*, 73; Witt, "Creation," 215–48.

38. See Blacketer, "Arminius' Concept of Covenant," 198–203.

39. Arminius, "Oration II," 1:349, 360.

40. Ibid., 1:362–67.

41. Ibid., 1:362; Arminius, *Opera Theologica*, 41: "*commodissime finis Theologiae adpellari potest, unio Dei cum homine.*"

42. Arminius, "Oration II," 1:362.

43. Witt, "Creation," 236.

The Views of Free Choice in the Prelapsarian State

the process of uniting himself with man such that something(s) of the true nature of God became part of the true nature of man.

One should note that, unlike Arminius, Calvin is very reticent to speak about union with God apart from Christ. It is not that Calvin does not believe that the highest blessedness for man finds its fulfillment in union with God. He does affirm, for example, that the perfection of the soul "consists in being united to God."[44] The preponderance of the times that he talks about union with God, he does so with reference to Christ. For example, Calvin tells us, "The Lord very frequently addresses us in the character of a husband; the union by which he connects us with himself, when he receives us into the bosom of the Church."[45]

Now, who is the God that unites himself with human beings? God is "the best and greatest of beings."[46] This God is one who is immutable in his nature and will.[47] God possesses understanding and will as part of his nature.[48] In addition, God has free will—*libera voluntas*[49] and *liberum arbitrium*.[50] This is the God who unites himself with man. In significant ways, for Arminius, man is like a small replica and microcosm of God with regard to the faculties of the soul and its function—truths that Psalm 8:5 seem to be communicating.

When does this union between God and man take place? Though there are two answers to this question—the second of which involves union with God and Christ—I focus only on the first one at this time. The union between God and man takes place at the time of creation when God creates man in his own image. In his disputation on the creation of man in the image of God, after stating that man, consisting of body and soul, is created

---

44. Calvin, *Institutes*, I.xv.6; see II.i.5.

45. Ibid., II.viii.18.

46. Arminius, "Oration II," 1:366.

47. Ibid., 1:367. On the question of God's immutability, the theology of Arminius is in conflict with the theology of established Arminianism, as Sanders understands it, and with open theism.

48. Arminius, "Public," 2:118–21; Arminius, "Private," 2:340–44.

49. Arminius, "Oration III," 1:376–77; idem, *Opera Theologica*, 47: "*contigentiae principium, libera voluntas Dei* [the principle of contingency is the free will of the Deity]." When talking about the complex necessity that exist in God and the creature, Arminius states, "*Verum in Deo . . . partim ex principio voluntatis liberae ipsius* [It truly is in God . . . partly on account of the principle of his free will]. See also Arminius, "Junius," 3:43.

50. Arminius, "Perkins's," 3:347; idem, *Opera Theologica*, 347: "*Deo liberum esse illam communicare pro arbitrio* [it is free to God to communicate that according to his own choice]."

in the image of God (*imago Dei*), Arminius mentions the received division of the soul into faculties of understanding and will and then says, "In all these things, the image of God most wonderfully shone forth: We say that this [*similitudo*] is the likeness by which man resembled his Creator, and expressed it according to the mode of his capacity: In his *soul*, according to its substance, faculties and habits."[51] The creation of man—making him in God's image—is an act of grace.

With respect to the *imago Dei* as such, Arminius makes a distinction between man created naturally (with the essential part of man without which he cannot be man) and supernaturally (with the accidental/nonessential part of man that is added). The natural part of man's creation consists of those things—soul and body—without which man cannot be man. Now, within the soul there is "the understanding [*intellectum*], and the will [*voluntatem*], and the liberty of the will [*voluntatisque libertatem*],[52] and other affections . . . which necessarily flow from them."[53] In contrast to the natural, the supernatural part consists of further knowledge, righteousness, and holiness that God adds to assist man in moving toward perfection.[54] These supernaturals are attributes that human beings share with the Divine nature. Arminius cites 2 Peter 1:4 to support this sharing in the Divine nature and he cites Colossians 3 (v. 10) and Ephesians 4 (vv. 23–24) in order to prove his selection of what constitutes the supernaturals. Similar to Calvin, he argues that whatever human beings have gained by regeneration in the Spirit are the supernaturals.[55] Initially, Arminius says that the image of God is located in the supernatural part. However, he later includes the natural (soul and body) into the image of God and further clarifies that the natural (essential) parts of man, without the supernatural (accidental)

---

51. Arminius, "Private," 2:363. Coming at the matter slightly differently he says, "It is natural and essential to the soul to be a spirit, and to be endowed with the power of understanding and of willing, both according to nature and the mode of liberty" (ibid.).

52. Here is an example of an interchangeable us of *voluntas* and *arbitrium*. It appears that Arminius uses these terms much more interchangeably than Calvin does. This may be so since, for Arminius, the will and its ability to choose are essentially and inextricably joined so that, for him, speaking of *libertatem voluntatis* is essentially the same as speaking of *liberum arbitrium*.

53. Arminius, "Junius," 3:112–13; idem, *Opera Theologica*, 410. A few pages over he speaks of "soul, mind, affection, and will" as the parts of the naturals/essentials (ibid., 118). Note that soul is here listed separately.

54. Arminius, "Junius," 3:113.

55. Ibid.

parts, by themselves do not constitute the image of God.[56] Now, it is significant at this point to note clearly that it is in the natural part—the part that is essential to man—that Arminius locates free choice (*liberum arbitrium*).

Therefore, picking up on the discussion of man's union with God, since God has created man in his image, man too has the faculty of will (*voluntas*) and the moral capacity to exercise his free choice (*arbitrium*) aright in the state of innocence. In one disputation, when talking about the idea of God permitting man to sin in the prelapsarian states, Arminius speaks of "The liberty of choosing [*libertas arbitrii*], with which God formed his rational creature, and which his constancy does not suffer to be abolished, lest he should be accused of mutability."[57] Though in this statement it is Arminius's intent to address free choice after the fall (postlapsarian), he nonetheless affirms that God created man initially with free choice. We also see here that God's twofold love for justice and for humankind may not be the leading theme in Arminius's theology, as den Boer claims.[58] Prior to the justice of God, which is an *ad extra* or economic attribute, there is the *ad intra* or immanent attributes of the immutability and constancy of God. Therefore, the immutability of God may well be the main theme in Arminius's theology from which his views on free choice and other theological topics are naturally derived. Clarke, Gerrit J. Hoenderdaal, Hicks, and Bangs all agree that Arminius affirms free choice in the prelapsarian state.[59]

When he gives his reasons for opposing supralapsarian predestination[60] in his "Declaration of Sentiments," Arminius points out that the

---

56. Ibid., 3:109–18, 153, 161, 439. Arminius will argue that in the fall the naturals were corrupted while the supernaturals were taken away. Note also that when understood in a certain restricted sense, as a homonym, "naturals" may refer to both the naturals and the supernaturals (ibid., 112).

57. Arminius, "Public," 2:167; idem, *Opera Theologica*, 201. See also idem, "Declaration," 1:659.

58. Boer, *God's Twofold Love*, 69; idem, "Jacobus Arminius," 25, 31, 40. In the article here cited, den Boer says, "In my opinion, the safeguarding of God's justice even forms the most important theme and context from which his [Arminius's] entire theology must be understood" (p. 31).

59. Clarke, "Theology of Arminius," 249; Hoenderdaal, "Debate," 138; Hicks, "Theology of Grace," 29 (Hicks says, "Arminius indomitably insists that the sin of Adam was a free act on his part which was unfettered by any kind of necessity. Free will was capable of evil without any necessary compulsion from within or without"); Bangs, *Arminius*, 197.

60. By "supralapsarian predestination" I mean that decree of God whereby he has decreed the salvation of the elect and the damnation of the reprobate prior to his decree to create the world and to permit the fall of man. Infralapsarianism, on the other hand, teaches that God's decree to save the elect and damn the reprobate was subsequent to his

doctrine is "contrary to the nature of man" that God "created with freedom of choice [*libero arbitrio*]" after "his own image."[61] Arminius's point here is not to imply that supralapsarians do not affirm the freedom of choice prior to and in the fall. Rather, his intent is to affirm that freedom of choice, which God created in man as an essential component, and *which persists after the fall*, is undermined by supralapsarian predestination.

With his free choice, according to Arminius, man is able genuinely to choose between good and evil. He is at liberty to obey and not to obey God. If this were not the case, it would have been absurd for God to command man not to eat from the tree of the knowledge of God and evil (Gen 1:17).[62] As we saw with Calvin, man is under no compulsion to act one way or the other. I would, therefore, agree with Dell's assessment that, for Arminius, free choice primarily meant "freedom from necessity, whether this proceeds from an external cause compelling, or a nature inwardly determining to absolutely one thing."[63] No eternal decree of God compels man to sin. In Arminius's understanding, Calvin's and Beza's views of the eternal decree of God necessarily lead to the conclusion that man was compelled to sin, having been deprived of genuine free choice even in the prelapsarian state by virtue of God's decree that determines all things.[64] Arminius's intent is to distance himself from Calvin and Beza's deterministic view of the divine decrees while maintaining man's freedom of contrary choice and the existence of genuine contingency. In addition to not being compelled to sin by a decree of God that determines the fall, man is predisposed positively—though not coerced—to choose the good.

---

decree to create and permit the fall.

61. Arminius, "Declaration," 1:625. In his *Opera*, Arminius opines that the doctrine of predestination is "contrary to the nature of man . . . whom God has created with free will." As he puts it, "*doctrina talis de Praedestinatione pugnat cum natural hominis, tam respectu eius quod creatas est ad imaginem Dei cum agnitione Dei & iustitia; quam quod creatas est cum libero arbitrio*" (Armini, *Opera Theologica*, 86).

62. Arminius, "Private," 2:369.

63. Dell, "Man's Freedom," 8. In his "Public Disputations," Arminius describes the freedom that the will possesses in five senses. In brief, there is freedom from control by another, freedom from the government of a superior, freedom from internal or external necessity (genuine choices exist), freedom from sin and its dominion, and freedom from misery. In his explanation of these five senses, Arminius points out that the first two apply only to God while the last three apply to man and were true of him as he was originally created (Arminius, "Public," 2:190).

64. Arminius, "Junius," 3:74, 76–77, 80–82.

The Views of Free Choice in the Prelapsarian State

In this state of primitive innocence, man is able to do good things that are truly pleasing to God. Arminius puts it this way: "In his primitive condition as he came out of the hands of his Creator, man was endowed with such a portion of knowledge, holiness, and power, as enabled him to understand, esteem, consider, will, and to perform the true good."[65] Man can do true spiritual good because he is endowed with true righteousness and holiness—the contents of the supernatural gifts. As Arminius states it, man "had a heart imbued . . . with a true and saving love of good; and powers abundantly qualified or furnished perfectly to fulfill the law which God had imposed on him."[66] In this state, "the will has an inclination to good," with the chief good being union with God.[67] Though man has a free choice that is inclined to do good, he also has the permission to commit sin.[68] In Arminius's thinking, for permission to be real permission, God must suspend his efficiency through his providential concurrence.[69] In this suspension of his efficiency, God chooses not to exercise his authority and power to the extent that he can do. He restrains himself. Had God exercised all the efficiency possible to him by way of right or ability, he could have prevented the free choice acts of man. Man, therefore, is able to have free choice because God suspends the full expression of his possible efficiency. The idea that God suspends his efficiency need not be understood in any sense that would take away from the glory, majesty, and power of God. All Arminius intends to say here is that God could have created man without this permission to sin, which God was free to do, just as Jesus was free to have called ten thousand angels to set himself free (Matt 26:53).

Therefore, the cause of the fall is found primarily in the Divine permission—as opposed to determination—given to the human will to sin. In the place of his "Public Disputations" where Arminius talks about the first sin and its cause, the primary phrase that he uses is *libera sua voluntate*. As Arminius puts it, "The efficient cause of this [first] sin is . . . Man himself, who, of his own free will [*libera sua voluntate*] and without any necessity either internal or external . . . transgressed the law which was proposed to him . . . and which it was possible for him to have observed."[70] Notwithstanding, he

---

65. Arminius, "Declaration," 1:659.
66. Arminius, "Public," 2:191.
67. Arminius, "Private," 2:363.
68. Arminius, "Public," 2:167.
69. Arminius, "Perkins's," 3:390, 418.
70. Arminius, "Public," 2:152; idem, *Opera Theologica*, 193. See idem, *Opera*

links free choice with the permission granted to the will such that man's free choice is the cause of the fall. Here he quotes Tertullian approvingly, saying, "If God had once allowed to man the free exercise of his own choice [*arbitrii libertatem*] and had duly granted this permission, he undoubtedly had permitted the enjoyment of those things through the very authority of the institution."[71] Here, Arminius ties free choice with the permission to sin—a permission God grants through the suspension of his divine efficiency.

One of the major concerns of Arminius, like that of Calvin, is to defend the justice of God by deflecting the charge that God is the author of sin.[72] In Arminius's way of thinking, in order for God to remain free from the charge, it is necessary for God to create man with free choice. It is this freedom of will and choice and their misuse that renders man inexcusable before God. Thus, by creating man with such freedom of choice, God limits himself with respect to creaturely contingency.[73] When I speak of contingency, I have in mind unnecessary occurrences that fall within the realm of the possible. Perhaps with the exception of our natural birth and death and the involuntary functions of the body, all of man's activity, e.g., going to the grocery store today to buy milk, falls within the realm of contingency. Certainly, God could have created a creature that is determined in every possible way like a preprogrammed robot. However, God could not have done so, on account of his immutability, and he chose not to do so for the sake of justice. Contingency and free choice necessarily relate to each other with free choice being one of the manifestations or outworking of contingency.

Since man has free choice and since the cause of the fall involves the will more than the intellect, is Arminius then a voluntarist? In answering this question, Arminius's view of God's relation to the creature plays an important role. God, in Arminius's view, already has an intellectualist predisposition.[74] At the moment of union between God and man in creation, we begin to see an intellectualism in Arminius's thought. He says, for example, "By this union, the understanding beholds in the clearest vision, and as if 'face to face,' God himself, and all his goodness and incomparable beauty."[75] Witt would later conclude that this clear vision is the beatific vision of the

---

Theologica, 151; idem, "Public," 2:162, 164.

71. Arminius, "Public," 2:154; idem, *Opera Theologica*, 194.
72. Arminius, "Apology," 1:762; idem, "Junius," 3:44, 76–77; idem, "Perkins's," 3:342.
73. Dell, "Man's Freedom," 144, 221, 228.
74. Muller, *God, Creation*, 145, 156, 165.
75. Arminius, "Oration II," 1:362–63.

Thomistic tradition.[76] In this union, the transcendent God naturally accommodates himself to human capacity, which results in an "extension of the understanding" and "an enlargement of the will."[77] Note that the union first affects the understanding.

When speaking about the will of God, he says, for example, "the act of the understanding [of God] is to offer it [known good] as a good to the will . . . that it [the will] may also discharge its office and act concerning this known good."[78] Thus, even in the life of God, the understanding presents to the will what the understanding deems good, so that the will may rationally decide to act on the basis of the good presented by the understanding.

Hence, since we are united with God by virtue of creation, it is only natural then to expect this intellectualism, which is in God the Creator, to be in the creature as well. The intellectual activity is always prior in the prelapsarian state in Arminius. It is the understanding that "beholds in the clearest vision . . . all his [God's] goodness and incomparable beauty."[79]

Though Arminius locates the cause of sin in the will (*libera voluntas*) and its choice (*arbitrium*), the will still acts in subjection to the intellect, which was persuaded to choose the path of disobedience, thinking that disobeying God was for the good of man (*sub specie bonitatis*). Man perceived an advantage in becoming like God, as the devil proposed, and took it. Therefore, the will followed that bad judgment of the deceived intellect.[80]

In much of this discussion thus far, Arminius is mirroring the views of Thomas Aquinas and the Thomistic tradition on these matters. Muller shows that Arminius used various Catholic sources that influenced his theology.[81] In one article, Muller argues that the reason creation plays such an important part in Arminius's theology "lies in [Arminius's] acceptance of a Thomistic conception of creation as an emanation of the divine potency for being and of the existence of the created order by participation in the goodness of divine being."[82] Certainly, this thought also applies elsewhere. The point here, however, is to show that Arminius was deeply influenced by the Thomistic tradition. Witt, in my judgment, exploits this connection to make Arminius

---

76. Witt, "Creation," 259.
77. Arminius, "Oration II," 1:363.
78. Arminius, "Public," 2:125.
79. Arminius, "Oration II," 1:362.
80. Arminius, "Public," 2:152–53.
81. Muller, "Scholastic," 268–71.
82. Muller, "God, Predestination," 440.

appear more Roman Catholic than is warranted,[83] as he, ironically, chides Bangs and Hicks for making Arminius into a "liberal Calvinist."[84]

As we will see, Arminius's view, which is similar to that of Aquinas, of the relationship between nature and grace will also have implications for how he understands the nature and function of the will in man's fallen, redeemed, and glorified states.

Conclusion Concerning Prelapsarian State

Though there are some similarities between Calvin and Arminius with respect to the function of the will in the prelapsarian state, these similarities are like similar icing daubed on two separate cakes made with quite different ingredients. Both agree that the misuse of man's free choice caused the fall. However, when we consider the reasons for the existence of free will and the nature of free will, we have seen that Arminius disagrees with Calvin at a fundamental level in the prelapsarian state, for Arminius locates the free choice of man in the soul as part of its necessary and natural makeup. For Calvin, free choice is not a natural and necessary part of the soul but an added component. This basic disagreement has significant ramifications that follow man into his other states of existence.

We have seen that Calvin limits his discussions about union with God in the prelapsarian state because, for him, such union takes places ultimately in Christ. For Calvin, creation in the image of God is about representation; man represents God. Therefore, I would disagree with Witt's assessment that Calvin's difficulty lies in his inability to give a correct expression to the distinction between God and the world. Witt may disagree with Calvin's way of relating God to the world; but this is no proof of error on Calvin's part. I concur then with Schreiner and Laytham, respectively, that the function of creation in Calvin's theology is to display God's glory and to render man inexcusable before God.

Creation, however, serves a different function for Arminius. As Witt correctly points out, for Arminius the goal of man's creation is union with God. Arminius considers this union to have already begun at creation, apart from reference to Christ. Arminius is not reticent to speak about union with God apart from Christ, as is the case with Calvin. For Arminius, creation in

---

83. Witt, "Creation," 203–4, 259, 268, 419.
84. Ibid., 193–94.

the image of God is primarily about union with God. It's not mainly about God displaying his glory or about rendering man inexcusable.

How this union with God takes place also highlights more differences. We may say of Calvin's position that God *communicates* himself to us by creating us in his image *with* intellect and will. However, for Arminius, we may say in creation God *unites* himself with us insofar as man's creaturely capacity allows. What is the difference? To *communicate* connotes giving or sharing without necessarily implying partial or total identity. To *unite* connotes giving and sharing by way of identification or participation. To use an analogy, it appears that in Arminius's view, the divine Painter becomes, in part, part of the painting. This analogy, however, ought not to be pressed to the point of suggesting that Arminius holds to pantheism or panentheism. It appears that, for Arminius, God creates man in his image by way of emanation.[85] By contrast, for Calvin, though the painting bears the mark of the divine Painter, the Painter *qua* Painter is completely distinct from the painting.

On the question of the *imago Dei*, more properly, there is also some disagreement over what exactly constitutes the image of God in man. For Calvin the image of God is primarily the supernatural gifts, which have to do with the right exercise or use of the natural gifts of intellect and will. For Arminius, on the other hand, the image of God in man includes both the natural and supernatural gifts.

The matter of the right use of the natural gifts brings the matter of free choice to the fore. Both Calvin and Arminius agree that man was created with a predisposition to do good but with the free choice to do evil. Both believe that man's choice is free. However, they differ on how free choice exists in man and on the kind of relationship that exists between the faculty of free will and the function of free choice.

For both Calvin and Arminius, the creation of man with free choice in the prelapsarian state renders null and void the charge that God is the author of sin. Calvin, however, would add that the rectitude and perfection with which man was created also serve to absolve God from the charge of being the author of sin. Arminius and Witt, however, would contend that Calvin's view of divine sovereignty cannot logically withstand the charge that God is the author of sin. Nevertheless, both Calvin and Arminius acknowledge that the blame for the fall must be attributed to man's misuse of his free will and choice.

---

85. Cf. Muller, "God, Predestination," 440.

On the matter of voluntarism versus intellectualism, though their purposes and conclusions are different, we see that Muller and Hoitenga are correct in affirming, respectively, that Arminius and Calvin hold to the priority of the intellect in the prelapsarian state.[86] However, Calvin switches to voluntarism in order to explain the fall. Both Arminius and Calvin attribute the cause of the fall to man's misuse of his free will and choice. But unlike the obedient will following the deceived intellect in Arminius, for Calvin, the will acted in disregard to the better judgment of the intellect.

---

86. Muller, "Priority," 65–67, 71; Hoitenga, *John Calvin*, 45–46.

Chapter 2

The Views of Free Choice in the Postlapsarian State

Calvin: Man's Choice is Limitedly Free and Primarily Bound

IF CALVIN AND ARMINIUS are by and large in agreement concerning the existence of free choice and its misuse in the fall of man in the prelapsarian state—with some significant differences relating to the manner and nature of its existence—other substantial differences emerge as we examine their views of man's will in the postlapsarian state.

The heart of the issue may be summarized in terms of continuities and discontinuities with respect to man in the fallen state in contrast to man as he was originally created. Does man still have the free choice to choose equally between good and evil? Does he have the freedom to accept or reject that gospel? On the other hand, is man determined in such a way that his eternal destiny is completely outside of his hands? If he responds favorably to the proffered gospel, does he contribute to his salvation by cooperating with God? And, what of the priority of the intellect; does this priority continue in the fallen state?

On the subject of free choice (*liberum arbitrium*), based on Calvin's response to Pighius, entitled, *Defensio sanae et orthodoxae doctrinae de servitute et liberatione humani arbitrii adversus calumnias Alberti Pighii Campensis*,[1] one *may assume* Calvin believes equally in bondage of choice

---

1. Translated as "A Defense of the Sound and Orthodox Doctrine of the Bondage and Liberation of Human Choice against the Calumnies of Albert Pighius of Kampen" (Lane, *Student*, 151, 179).

and free choice in the post-fall state.[2] Though the issues addressed in *Defensio sanae et orthodoxae . . . Campensis* are more complex and belie such easy categorization, one could argue that Lane seems to lean in that direction when he claims that to try to ascertain whether Calvin believes in free will (choice) definitively is a work in futility, considering that Calvin himself argued different points of the issue depending upon his audience at the time.[3] That there is development in Calvin's treatment of the will in the *Institutes* due to interaction with various opponents makes Lane's view seem plausible.[4] On the other hand, Leith makes the comment that "the one point on which Calvin is adamant is that fallen man does not have freedom of contrary choice in relationship to God."[5]

In his contribution to the discussion, Bruce R. Reichenbach asserts, "The freedom asserted by Calvin and the compatibilist is an illusion, for the coercion that controls our acts when we are not free here extends to our desires and choices."[6] Reichenbach's motive in arguing for freedom in opposition to divine sovereignty is to make man morally accountable and responsible—goals that Calvin's idea of divine sovereignty seems to undermine. How can a person be punished for a crime he could not help but commit?

Paul Helm's position supports the view of Leith. In response to Vincent Brümmer, who joins Hoitenga in pointing out inconsistencies in Calvin's teaching, Helm states very clearly that "Calvin's view is much more radical; it is that the loss of free will to do good is such that even when a person has the knowledge of the will of God he does not will [choose] to do it."[7] Brümmer argues that Calvin is inconsistent because he initially advocates the natural indestructibility of free will (choice) and then later sacrifices free choice for the sake of efficacious grace and the perseverance of the saints. But Brümmer is being imprecise in his analysis here since he apparently

---

2. The issue may be otherwise. It may be that though free choice remains within the limitation of the will in sin—that is, the will is bound in sin—man's bound will still freely chooses individual acts. An unredeemed sinner, for example, may voluntarily/freely choose not to steal from his neighbor as a merely external act. Nevertheless, this unredeemed sinner will always choose not to steal sinfully because his external act of not stealing was not done through the influences of a renewed mind and a change heart.

3. Lane, "Did Calvin?," 86.

4. See Schulze, "Calvin's Defense," 165.

5. Leith, "Doctrine," 53.

6. Reichenbach, "Freedom, Justice," 283; cf. 299.

7. Helm, "Reply," 462; see Brümmer, "Calvin, Bernard," 449–50, 452–54; Witt, "Creation," 98; Hoitenga, *John Calvin*, 14.

has failed to properly distinguish the faculty of free will from the function of free will. Calvin indeed advocates the indestructability of the faculty of free will, but clearly teaches that the free choice function of the will is a gift that can be taken away. So, as we will see more clearly below, there is no real inconsistency on Calvin's part on this point.

Though for different reasons than Brümmer, Hoitenga argues that Calvin inconsistently moves from prelapsarian intellectualism in the fallen state to voluntarism in the redeemed state. Calvin fails the test of consistency a second time, according to Hoitenga, by teaching simultaneously that man's natural gifts are not taken away and that these gifts are so corrupt that man can will and do no good.[8] One wonders why this is an inconsistency! All Calvin means to say here is that the corruption of the gifts so affects their proper function that it is as if those gifts have been taken away. A car may have all the natural mechanical abilities to function as a car, but if one is deprived of its proper use because of tainted gas, it is as if fuel has been completely removed from the car, which makes it no good as a car. The adulteration and corruption of fuel, to use a related example, makes the fuel unusable, in which case, it is as if the fuel has been completely taken away. Examples of this reality abound. Of what use is corrupted wine, or a vacuum without the electricity to run it?

Another possible response to Brümmer and Hoitenga may be found in D. Brent Laytham and others, for whom apparent logical inconsistencies are not great surprises in Calvin, since his purpose is to be faithful to biblical revelation rather than human logic. In assessing Calvin's approach to theology in general, Laytham says, "Rather than a closed system, he works with 'a whole series of Biblical ideas, some of which can only with difficulty be logically reconciled.'"[9] Laytham further claims that the inconsistencies in Calvin are "merely formal" since "Calvin logically reconciles their content."[10]

My own view is that when free will (i.e. free choice) is understood in the sense of freedom from necessity—without the connotation of compulsion or coercion—and the ability to choose between spiritual good and evil in the fallen state, Calvin clearly teaches that man's will is in a state of bondage. To use Dell's words, "Calvin opposes the notion that sinful man

---

8. Hoitenga, *John Calvin*, 45–50, 69–80.

9. Laytham, "Natural Theology," 23–24. On the matter of logical inconsistency in Calvin, see Wendel, *Calvin*, 357–58; Leith, "Calvin's Theological Method," 107; Armstrong, "*Duplex*," 136; Partee, "Determinism," 128.

10. Laytham, "Natural Theology," 36.

has free will."[11] The context of this quotation from Dell makes it quite clear that Dell has in mind free will in the sense of freely choosing (*liberum arbitrium*) the good, which would result in meriting salvation.

How does Calvin work this out? He acknowledges that the *imago Dei* in man "was not utterly effaced and destroyed . . . ; it was, however, *so corrupted*, that anything which remains is fearful deformity."[12] I believe that Calvin is thinking of *imago Dei* here in the broader sense (which includes the creation of the soul with its faculties), since he later argues that the image of God is properly related to the supernatural gifts, which are *not corrupted* but taken away. Nevertheless, in Calvin's understanding, a radical change takes place in man after the fall. This change is so radical that Calvin likens the estrangement of the soul to death—a death that entails the soul's total corruption in every part. Man's intellect and will are "defiled and pervaded with . . . concupiscence."[13]

However, this corruption of man does not proceed from man's originally created nature. Though the corruption is still natural in the sense that this is what we have naturally become due to the fall, it is not part of man as he was originally created.[14] To bring clarity, Calvin uses the Aristotelian distinction between substantial and accidental qualities. He argues that the corruption of nature results from the accidental character of the fall, viewed from the perspective of man as he was created, and not from the nature of the "substantial property assigned to him from the beginning."[15] Granted, from the perspective of God's decree, the fall is not accidental. The point is that though God ordained the fall, the fall and resulting corruption did not come about due to natural necessity—that is, some inherent condition or quality within the nature of man. As we will see more clearly below, the fall did not result from a defect in man's nature but from man's voluntary misuse of his free choice. However, even in fallen and corrupt creatures the faculties of the soul remain; yet their proper functions are severely altered,

---

11. Dell, "Man's Freedom," 51. See Schulze, "Calvin's Reply to Pighius," 180.
12. Calvin, *Institutes*, I.xv.4 (emphasis added); Calvin, *Ezekiel*, 11:375, 376.
13. Calvin, *Institutes*, II.i.8, 5; see II.iii.2.
14. Ibid., II.i.11; Calvin, *Bondage*, 40.
15. Calvin, *Institutes*, II.i.11. This use of these distinctions is contrary to Hoitenga's claim that Calvin does not use Aristotelian "minutiae." When it serves his purposes, Calvin does borrow from the philosophers so long as the concepts borrowed do not obscure but help to clarify the biblical truth (Hoitenga, *John Calvin*, 24); see Calvin, *Institutes*, I.xv.4, 7.

thus making the soul "incapable of one righteous desire."¹⁶ Hence, there is no inclination in man to do good but only evil continually. Man's will is "bound by the fetters of sin"¹⁷ and as such is dead.¹⁸

The severe damage done to the soul in the fall, Calvin affirms, results from the corruption of the natural gifts, which is due to the supernatural gifts having been withdrawn.¹⁹ By the supernatural gifts, Calvin means "the light of faith and righteousness, which would have been sufficient for the attainment of heavenly life and everlasting felicity."²⁰ The natural gifts are the faculties of the intellect and the will by themselves, separate from their function. However, though the natural gifts are retained after the fall, they are severely corrupted. In this corruption, as Calvin puts it, "*soundness* of mind and *integrity* of heart were, at the same time, withdrawn, and it is this which constitutes the corruption of the natural gifts."²¹ The natural gifts become corrupted *because* the supernatural gifts have been removed.

This "fearful deformity" of the soul results in the loss of man's free choice, among other things. In response to the sixth session of the Council of Trent, Calvin maintains, "If the will [*voluntas*] were wholly depraved, its health would not only be impaired but lost until it were renewed."²² The will's (*voluntas*) health that is lost is the ability to choose freely—the function that the supernatural gifts makes possible—between good and evil without necessity. To Christians in general, Calvin writes,

> But those who, while they profess to be the disciples of Christ, still seek for free-choice [*liberum arbitrium*] in man, notwithstanding of his being lost and drowned in spiritual destruction, labor under manifold delusion, making a heterogeneous mixture of inspired doctrine and philosophical opinions, and so erring as to both.²³

16. Calvin, *Institutes*, II.ii.12.

17. Ibid., II.ii.7.

18. Calvin, *Ezekiel*, 11:375, 376.

19. Calvin, *Institutes*, II.ii.12. There is an apparent similarity to Arminius in Arminius, "Junius," 3:116.

20. Calvin, *Institutes*, II.ii.12.

21. Ibid., II.ii.12.

22. Calvin, *Selected Works*, 109; *Calvini, Opera Omnia*, 7:443.

23. Calvin, *Institutes*, I.xv.8; *Calvini, Opera Omnia*, 2:143. In his sermons on Deuteronomy, Calvin says, "*Ainsi donc apprenons de ne nous plus abuser en ces folles imaginations, cuidans avoir franc-arbitre de ceci ou de cela* [So then, let us learn to deceive ourselves no more with these fond imaginations, in thinking ourselves to have free choice to do this or that]" (ibid, 26:647; Calvin, *Sermons on Deuteronomy*, 377).

In other words, Christians who believe in free choice after the fall are neither good theologians nor good philosophers. In further response to Trent, Calvin says,

> Let us remember, therefore, that will [*voluntatem*] in man is one thing, and the free choice [*liberam . . . electionem*] of good and evil another: for freedom of choice [*eligendi liberate*] having been taken away after the fall of the first man, will [*voluntas*] alone was left; but so completely captive under the tyranny of sin, that it is only inclined to evil.[24]

Here, Calvin makes a specific distinction between free choice and the faculty of will, reaffirming the status quo that the faculty of will is not destroyed.[25] Thus, Brümmer's assertion that Calvin later advocated the destruction of free will after advocating its indestructibility is incorrect; at best, his analysis is confusing. What has been destroyed is the ability to use rightly the faculty of will. Calvin also implies that there is a distinction between free choice of good and evil and free choice of committing or not committing particular acts—acts which when committed are still committed sinfully.

However, though the free choice of man, properly understood, is taken away, Calvin insists that man is still limitedly free, in the sense that man is a voluntary slave to sin, and as such sins necessarily but without compulsion or coercion. However, Calvin would rather not dignify man in his fallen state "with so proud a title" of free choice (*liberi arbitrii*)—even if doing so serves to render man inexcusable before God.[26] For Calvin, that man was created in an upright state and fell of his own free choice, that he still has a will, that he lives in a world which displays God's glory in every part, and that the law is written upon his conscience all make him inexcusable before God. As Calvin says,

> The end [purpose] of the natural law, therefore, is to render man inexcusable, and may be not improperly defined—the judgment of conscience distinguishing sufficiently between just and unjust, and by convicting men on their own testimony depriving them of all pretext for ignorance.[27]

---

24. Calvin, *Selected Works*, 113; *Calvini, Opera Omnia*, 7:446. *Electio* means choice or election (Stelten, *Dictionary*, 85).

25. Calvin, *Ezekiel*, 11:379; Calvin, *Institutes*, II.ii.12; II.iii.5, 6. See also Calvin, *Sermons on Deuteronomy*, 1053.

26. Calvin, *Institutes*, II.ii.7; *Calvini, Opera Omnia*, 2:191.

27. Calvin, *Institutes*, II.ii.22. See also Calvin, *Sermons on Deuteronomy*, 1053;

The Views of Free Choice in the Postlapsarian State

Though he dislikes the proud title, when understood a certain way—a way in which it is not generally understood—and in a very restrictive sense, Calvin makes use of the title to describe the limited sense in which man has free choice when he says, "In this way, then, man is said to have free choice [*liberi . . . arbitrii*], not because he has a free choice [*liberam . . . electionem*] of good and evil, but because he acts . . . voluntarily and not by compulsion."[28] In this sense, man has free will. And in this brief explanation, Calvin thus redefines how *liberum arbitrium*, when used, ought to be understood. Man sins voluntarily (freely) *and* necessarily.[29] In this sense, Calvin does not understand necessity to imply compulsion.[30]

To show that necessity does not necessarily entail compulsion and coercion, Calvin points out that God is necessarily good and the devil is necessarily evil.[31] Yet both God and the devil are freely good and evil, respectively. In one sense, then, the devil is free to do good and God is free to do evil just as the deer is free to be a carnivore. However, the nature of God and the nature of the devil necessarily constrain them to be who they are and act according to their natures. Therefore, God's own nature and character prevent him from being and doing evil. God can only be good. In his response to Pighius, Calvin says, "For we do not say that man is dragged unwillingly into sinning, but that because his will is corrupt he is held captive under the yoke of sin and therefore of necessity wills in an evil way. For where there is bondage, there is necessity."[32] Calvin continues and says, "We locate the necessity to sin precisely in corruption of the will, from which it follows that it is self-determined."[33] The will of man then is not compelled or coerced to sin by any external force and not even by God. The will of man sins willingly, i.e., freely or spontaneously.

In light of all of this, it follows that for Calvin fallen man can do no spiritual good. Man in his fallen state cannot seek after God nor seek after the things of God (Rom 3:10–12). Calvin admits, though, that man can

---

Calvini, Opera Omnia, 28:560: "*Or Dieu a imprimé en nous de nature une volonté: entant que nous sommes hommes, nous avons discretion du bien et du mal pour nous rendre inexcusables* [Indeed God has imprinted a will in us by nature and for as much as we are men, we have a discretion to discern good and evil]."

28. Calvin, *Institutes*, II.ii.7; *Calvini, Opera Omnia*, 2:191.
29. Calvin, *Institutes*, II.v.1.
30. Ibid., II.ii.5, 7; Helm, "Reply," 459–61.
31. Calvin, *Institutes*, II.iii.5.
32. Calvin, *Bondage*, 69.
33. ibid, 70.

do earthly good. Man can excel in the arts and be a good doctor or mechanic, etc. But for Calvin, this earthly good that man is able to do is a kind of inferior goodness.[34] Man may even live in outward conformity to the law.[35] Witt acknowledges this teaching of Calvin when he says, "there is still freedom, according to Calvin, in regard to things below."[36] Calvin even considers the natural inclination of the individual to pursue his happiness as a good thing; but this good results from a natural inclination for comfort rather than from a true righteous desire to live in conformity to God's will.[37] However, even such good inclination is not proof of human free choice. For, the unbeliever has completely lost the desire for the *true* good in the fall and is inclined to only evil.[38] Only those who have the Holy Spirit aspire to universal blessedness.[39] Certainly, the unbeliever desires "good" as his sinful nature guides him, so that he continues to commit sin as evil and under the guise of doing good (*sub specie bonitatis*).

After affirming that the chief good is union with God, Calvin points out that man "could not, however, form even an imperfect idea of its nature; nor is this strange, as he had learned nothing of the sacred bond of that union," and that one of the marks that set the believer apart from the unbeliever is the desire that the believer has for union with God.[40] Calvin maintains that, if by free choice one means the power to choose between good and evil, the term and idea must be rejected. But on the other hand, "If freedom is opposed to coercion," says the less dogmatic Calvin, "I both acknowledge and consistently maintain that choice is free, and I hold anyone who thinks otherwise to be a heretic."[41]

This loss of free choice in the sense of the power to choose between good and evil is a present reality despite God's continued providential

---

34. Calvin, *Institutes*, II.ii.13, 14, 15.

35. Calvin, *Romans*, 19:96–97; Calvin, *Institutes*, II.iii.3.

36. Witt, "Creation" 95.

37. Calvin, *Institutes*, II.ii.26.

38. Calvin, *Sermons on Deuteronomy*, 1016; *Calvini, Opera Omnia*, 28:491, "*si est-ce que de son propre mouvement, et de sa franche volonté (comme on dit) il sera tousiours attiré à mal, non point qu'il y soit forcé* [yet is it so, that of his own proper motion, and of his own free will (as they term it) he is always drawn unto evil]."

39. Calvin, *Institutes*, II.ii.26.

40. Ibid., III.xxv.2.

41. Calvin, *Bondage*, 68; *Calvini, Opera Omnia*, 6:279: "*Si coactioni opponitur libertas, liberum esse arbitrium, et fateor, et constanter assevero: ac pro haeretico habeo, quisquis secu sentiat.*"

activities in the world. Calvin holds a view of providence that keeps man's will in bondage. Calvin affirms that divine immutability guarantees that the fall will not frustrate God's purposes for creation.[42] Though God's purposes will not be frustrated, creation and the creature will be frustrated because of sin. Paul tells us in the book of Romans that the whole creation groans, waiting to be liberated with the sons of God (8:22), and that no one does good nor seeks after God (3:10–12). Therefore, this guarantee of preservation that God's immutability gives does not apply to man's free choice. As we will see, this is a significant point of difference between Calvin and Arminius.

Further support for fallen man's lack of free choice is seen in Calvin's teaching on providence. Here, Calvin teaches that nothing happens by fortune or chance, though, from a human perspective, mere chance and fortune seem to be operative in the world.[43] From God's perspective, since everything happens by his decree, there is no chance.[44] There are apparent chance happenings with man but not with God.[45] In Calvin's view of providence, God "holds the helm and overrules all events."[46] Therefore, "all the changes which take place in the world are produced by the secret agency of the hand of God."[47] In the final analysis, Calvin's articulation of the doctrine of providence buttresses his position for the bondage of the will.

When one considers all Calvin has to say regarding man's lack of free choice and God's decretal rule of all aspects of human life, it is logical to conclude that man is determined. Therefore, in light of Calvin's view on providence and grace, it is correct to say that Calvin is a determinist—a charge that Arminius will eventually bring against Calvin.[48] However, Calvin goes on to point out that necessity of nature, which is Stoic determinism, is not implied by his teaching of God's providence.[49] Though Calvin rejects the causal determinism of the Stoics, he goes on to espouse a different kind of determinism—a Divine determinism which stands in contrast to one that results from the inherent created nature of man. For, in the same passage

---

42. Calvin, *Institutes*, I.vii.12; Schreiner, *Theater*, 35.
43. Calvin, Institutes, I.xvi.9; Calvin, *Sermons on Deuteronomy*, 690.
44. Calvin, *Institutes*, I.xvi.2; I.xvi.4; I.xvi.9.
45. Ibid., I.xvi.9.
46. Ibid., I.xvi.4; I.xvii.1.
47. Ibid., I.xvi.9.
48. Witt, "Creation" 84, 85, 86, 89; Brümmer, "Calvin, Bernard," 451–55.
49. Calvin, *Institutes*, I.xvi.9.

where Calvin mentions the determinism of Stoics, he, with the same fervor displayed against Pighius, states, "Hence we maintain that, by providence, not heaven and earth and inanimate creatures only, but also the counsels and wills of men are so governed as to move exactly in the course which he [God] has destined."[50] Calvin further clarifies his view by appealing to distinctions made by the Schoolmen. He uses the example of Jesus's bones, which were left unbroken (John 19:36) not because of their nature (absolute or consequent necessity), but because of the decree of God (hypothetical or contingent necessity of consequence).[51] "Hence again," Calvin says, "we see that there was good ground for the distinction which the Schoolmen made between the necessity, *secundum quid* [relative], and necessity absolute, also between the necessity of consequent and of consequence."[52] Calvin also states that providence works with, without, and against means.[53] Therefore, for Calvin, contingencies exist from God's perspective, since, e.g., the soldiers could have broken Christ's bones but chose not to do so. In this sense, the fact of the soldiers not breaking Christ's bones is a contingent event since there was nothing in the nature of bones themselves that prevented them from being broken. However, these kinds of contingencies are not mere chance occurrences; they are foreordained means that God uses to bring man to his predetermined purposes. Calvin's view of contingency does not allow for a world in which man operates independently of God's foreordained plan and in which man by his choice determines his end.

Calvin acknowledges that there is providential grace operative in the fallen world.[54] He is not afraid of using the term "grace" positively to refer to this more general work of God in creation. Thus, when talking about the earthly good things that men do, Calvin points out that even this kind of good results from God's grace. In later theological development, this grace came to be known as "common grace."[55] Biblical support for this idea of grace is found in texts such as Matthew 5:45, which speaks of God sending the rain to fall on the just and on the unjust. However, though he readily uses "grace" to describe God's providential governance and sustenance of creation, which allows humankind to do earthly good, Calvin—contrary to Arminius as we

50. Ibid., I.xvi.8.
51. Ibid., I.xvi.9.
52. Ibid., I.xvi.9.
53. Ibid., I.xvii.1.
54. Bergvall, "Reason in Luther, Calvin," 120, 122; Calvin, *Institutes*, I.xvi.4; II.ii.15.
55. Berkhof, *Systematic Theology*, 432ff.

The Views of Free Choice in the Postlapsarian State

will see—finds the grace of providence (common grace) lacking in efficacy with respect to giving man the ability to exercise free choice in spiritual matters. Man can do no *spiritual* good apart from special, effectual, and saving grace given only to the elect.[56] The primary function of providential grace in Calvin's theology is, when dealing with human ability, to restrain sin.[57] God's providential (common) grace is operative in creation to keep man from living out the full potential of his evil nature, and not for the purpose of giving man power to do spiritual good works that are pleasing to God. In this case, common grace functions negatively. For man to be able to do spiritual good, he needs efficacious grace from God—a grace that is very different in quality from pre-fall grace and providential grace. As Calvin says it, "Seeing, then, that no good proceeds from us unless in so far as we are regenerated—and our regeneration is without exception wholly of God—there is no ground for claiming to ourselves one iota in good works."[58]

With this discussion of "general" grace in the background, we are in a better position to discuss issues relating to man's involvement or lack thereof in his salvation. When it comes to salvation, in Calvin's view, particular or special grace induces an irresistible positive response to the gospel.[59] One of the points Calvin makes in his *Institutes* is that the offer of the gospel in preaching and the sincere call to obedience do not imply that man has the free choice to respond and fulfill what has been commanded.[60] The power to respond comes from God. Quoting Augustine approvingly, Calvin says, "Let God give what he orders, and order what he wills."[61] Therefore, regeneration does not occur because man cooperates with God; regeneration is the sovereign work of God alone. Says Calvin, commenting on Philippians 1:6,

> There cannot be a doubt that, by the good work thus begun, he means the very commencement of conversion in the will. *God . . . begins* the good work in us by exciting in our hearts a desire, a love, and a study of righteousness, or (to speak more correctly) by turning, training, and guiding our hearts unto righteousness; and *he completes* this good work by confirming us unto perseverance.[62]

---

56. Calvin, *Institutes*, II.ii.6.
57. Ibid., II.iii.3; II.iii.2.
58. Ibid., III.xv.7.
59. Calvin's inconsistency, according to Brümmer, "Calvin, Bernard," 438–55.
60. Calvin, *Institutes*, II.ii.20; II.v.5; II.v.9; contra Arminius.
61. Ibid., II.v.7. See also Calvin, *Sermons on Deuteronomy*, 1052–54.
62. Calvin, *Institutes*, II.iii.6 (emphasis added).

Thus, the entirety of salvation is the work of God—a work in which the will does not simply cooperate but is charmed to submit and respond to efficacious grace. Calvin clearly rejects the distinction Arminius will make between various quantities of grace—designated as operating, preventing, cooperating, and subsequent grace—which "insinuates that man, by his own nature, desires good in some degree, though ineffectually."[63] When individuals respond and receive the special grace of God, it is not because they are cooperating with operating grace by exercising their free choice, which will lead to subsequent grace. Calvin says,

> This movement of the will [*voluntatem*] is not of that description which was for many ages taught and believed—viz. a movement which therefore leaves us the choice [*electionis*] to obey or resist it—but one which affects us efficaciously. We must, therefore, repudiate the oft-repeated sentiment of Chrysostom, 'Whom he draws, he draws willingly [*volentem*]'; insinuating that the Lord only stretches out his hand, and waits to see whether we will be pleased to take his aid. We grant that, as man was originally constituted, he could incline to either side, but since he has taught us by his example how miserable a thing free will [*liberum arbitrium*] is if God works not in us to will and to do, of what use to us were grace imparted in such scanty measure?[64]

For Calvin, then, God's irresistible and efficacious grace so overpowers the will of man, making him "heartily willing and ready, henceforth, to live unto God."[65] When it comes to salvation, saving grace does not simply make man able; it makes man's will willing. This grace causes man to believe. Calvin says,

> When the will is enchained as the slave of sin, it cannot make a movement towards goodness, far less steadily pursue it. Every such movement is the first step in that conversion to God, which in Scripture is entirely ascribed to divine grace. Thus Jeremiah prays, 'Turn thou me, and I shall be turned' (Jeremiah xxxi.18).[66]

On this issue, then, Calvin is a monergist who denounces cooperating with God's special grace, even apart from the added concern of co-earning. As Ephesians 2 teaches, human beings were dead in their trespasses and sin . . .

---

63. Ibid., II.ii.6; see II.iii.7.
64. Ibid., II.iii.10 (emphasis added); *Calvini, Opera Omnia*, 2:220.
65. Heidelberg Catechism, Lord's Day 1, Q&A 1.
66. Calvin, *Institutes*, II.iii.5.

but God who is rich in mercy made us alive in Christ, so that we have been saved solely by grace with the exclusion of every work on the part of man.

In light of all we have seen in Calvin's thought about the work of grace on the will,[67] it is very clear that, when it comes to salvation, he is a voluntarist. Prior to the fall, the will was able to select from the choices presented to it by the intellect. Then, there was a clear priority of intellect. However, in man's fallen condition, the issue of the priority becomes somewhat nebulous and distorted. At times, fallen man knows evil through reason but may justify doing the evil under the pretext of doing good (*sub specie bonitatis*). At other times, fallen man knowingly and willingly rushes to commit sin knowing that it is sin and evil.[68] Moreover, though it is still the office of reason to present the good to the will, reason is so weak and corrupt that it lacks coherence in spiritual matters.[69] Though there are still sparks by which man is distinguished as a rational creature from the lower animals, in matters of true religion, "human reason makes not the least approach."[70]

For Calvin, the moment sin is introduced into the equation of human existence, the voluntaristic position de facto asserts itself since sin has corrupted the functions of the intellect and will and the ordinary and proper relation that ought to exist between them. Calvin, then, may at this point be called a hamartiological voluntarist. This is a functional, not a thoroughgoing voluntarism. The transition from intellectualism begins in the garden, when the will chose to disregard right reason, follow the reasoning of the devil, and commit sin. This had to be the case since the intellect does not act; the will acts. This "voluntaristic crack," as Hoitenga calls it, which was opened to allow the fall, stays open even after the fall.[71] But this move from intellectualism to voluntarism is not illogical and inconsistent. As Calvin sees it, when one considers the massive effect of sin upon the human person, it is quite logical and consistent, biblically speaking, that there should be an equally severe negative effect upon the intellect and will. Were a meteor of sufficient size (say a quarter the size of the earth) and strength to

---

67. Calvin, *Ezekiel*, 12:264: "By the word *heart*, I understand him to mean the seat of all the affections; and by *spirit*, the intellectual part of the soul. The heart is often taken for the reason and intelligence; but when these two words are joined together, the spirit relates to the mind, and so it is the intellectual faculty of the soul; but the heart is taken for the will, or the seat of all the affections." See idem, *Institutes*, II.iii.6.

68. Calvin, *Institutes*, II.ii.23.

69. Ibid., II.ii.12.

70. Ibid., II.ii.12-19; see II.iii.1.

71. Hoitenga, *John Calvin*, 32.

strike the earth, one would expect that earth would be jolted and knocked off its course, even temporarily. It would be illogical and inconsistent to assume otherwise. Sin, in Calvin's mind, was a meteor of sufficient size that it jolted and knocked man off course such that normal priorities and functions were significantly affected.

Therefore, in the fallen state, the will no longer submits to reason, no longer waits upon reason, and no longer functions at reason's beck and call.[72] With the damage done to the intellect by original sin, the will is virtually left on its own to choose to act.[73] Also, complicating matters even more, the intellect does not always present true good to the will. In such a situation, the will responds to the depraved appetite of the flesh—sinful human nature.

Arminius: Man's Choice Is Limitedly Bound and Primarily Free

As was the case with Calvin, with Arminius, the bulk of the literature focuses upon various aspects of Arminius's postlapsarian teaching concerning the will.

With respect to Arminius's postlapsarian view of the will, as one would expect, opinions vary. Bryant claims that Arminius's advocacy of free will "is a well-documented fact of history."[74] Keep in mind that when I speak of free will, unless otherwise noted, I am really talking about free choice. Bangs, on the other hand, affirms that Arminius teaches that in the life of sin there is no free will.[75] Hoenderdaal, agreeing with Bangs, says Arminius discusses the free will of man in "true Reformation spirit," as he teaches the loss of free will, of purity, of moral strength, and of the ability to attain righteousness apart from grace." Hoenderdaal then concludes, "This is clearly Calvinist theology: there is no affinity with humanism or with Pelagianism"[76]—a statement with which Hicks, Clarke, and Roger Olson would concur.[77]

---

72. Calvin, *Institutes*, II.ii.27; II.iii.1.
73. Ibid., II.i.9.
74. Bryant, "Molina, Arminius," 96.
75. Bangs, *Arminius*, 191, 313, 341.
76. Hoenderdaal, "Debate," 138; see also 139. Incidentally, Hoenderdaal's claim does not exclude the semi-Pelagian option, though Olson's perspective of Arminius's teaching would.
77. Olson, *Arminian Theology*, 17–18.

The Views of Free Choice in the Postlapsarian State

As we have observed in the introduction, Witt, Hicks (who says, "Arminius does not believe that man in the fallen state possess a free will"), and Dell (who believes Arminius taught both bondage and freedom of the will) are all in disagreement over Arminius's view of the will.[78] For example, Witt would have us believe that where Protestant Scholasticism—of Beza, Perkins, Gomarus, and Turretin—failed to resolve the ambiguities of Calvin's thought, Arminius prevailed by being "able to relate creatively the distinction between creator and creature with an understanding of the risen Christ as the mediator of grace."[79]

On the issue of grace, Bangs and Witt believe Arminius is not a synergist, but a monergist who stands with the Reformers on the teaching of grace alone and the destitution of sinful man.[80] They agree and contend that since only cooperation is involved, devoid of the implication of co-earning, there is no synergism in Arminius.[81] This is a novel view of synergism since synergism is essentially cooperation. Thus, Olson, in opposition to Bangs and Witt, is able to maintain that Arminius is a synergist and further argues that the *evangelical* synergism of Arminius belongs in the realm of Protestant orthodoxy.[82] In addition, the argument has been advanced that Arminius departs from current Reformed doctrine in the area of theology proper, not in the area of anthropology.[83] In light of what we have already seen about Arminius's view of God and creation, particularly the creation man, a slight rephrasing of Hoenderdaal's thought is required at this point. Though the initial departure took place in the area of theology proper, that initial trickle of a breech flowed down the theological stream and became a raging flood that significantly undermined the foundations of Reformed orthodoxy's understanding of anthropology, which had only recently been fortified. So, there was a significant departure in the area of anthropology, which resulted from an apparent minor departure in the area of theology proper with regards to God's immutability and how that has been communicated to the creature. Therefore, contrary to these views, Sproul and Muller point out that, due to the ever-so-slight involvement of human choice in the matter of salvation,

---

78. Witt, "Creation," 203, 209, 419; Hicks, "Theology of Grace," 36, 32; Dell, "Man's Freedom," 148.

79. Witt, "Creation," 168.

80. Bangs, "Arminius and the Reformation," 164–66; Witt, "Creation," 660.

81. Bangs, "Arminius and Reformed Theology," 166–67.

82. Olson, *Arminian Theology*, 13–14, 18.

83. Hoenderdaal, "Debate," 138.

Arminius is a soteriological synergist (semi-Pelagian).[84] As Muller states it, Arminius's modified acceptance of "the late medieval dictum, *facere quod in se est, Deus non denegat gratiam*," makes him a synergist.[85] Stanglin, however, believes that Arminius's slight modification of adding grace to the first part of the medieval dictum clears him from being associated with the medieval synergistic understanding of the phrase.[86]

With these varying views in mind, I will advocate the position that Arminius believes man's will experiences limited bondage but is primarily and efficaciously free in its fallen condition. Again, one of Arminius's motives here is to avoid making God the immediate determinative cause of man's sin and rebellion[87] and, in so doing, to protect God's justice and goodness.[88] Any theological formulation that points in the direction of making God the author of sin is repugnant to Arminius's understanding of the nature and character and justice of God. Therefore, the main reason Arminius posits and defends human free will is not simply to advocate free will for its own sake and to dignify man with a proud title, but to protect the reputation of God. Olson has done a fine job in demonstrating that the main reason Arminius advocates the view that man has free will is for the purpose of protecting the goodness of God against what appears to the inevitable conclusion of Calvin's view, which makes God the author of sin. Arminius argues for free will not because of an a priori elevated view of human nature. His intention is not to siphon off some of God's glory and then transfer it to human beings so that they can think more highly of themselves than they ought to think. Arminius's primary concern is about God, not man. Therefore, I concur with Witt's summary at this point when he says, "Arminius' chief concern was to formulate adequately the theology of grace in a manner which preserves the integrity of the divine and the created orders while simultaneously embracing a christocentric theology of redemption."[89] Though I concur with

---

84. Sproul, *Willing to Believe*, 132; Muller, "Christological Problem," 157; Muller, "Gambit," 258, 261, 262.

85. Muller, "Federal Motif," 107; cf. 122. The modification of Arminius reads, "God will bestow more grace upon that man who does what is in him by the power of Divine Grace which is already granted to him, according to the declaration of Christ, To him that hath shall be given (Matt. Xiii, 11, 12)" (Arminius, "Apology," 2:16).

86. Stanglin, *Assurance*, 82–83.

87. Arminius, "Hippolytus," 2:700–701; Arminius, "Perkins's," 3:291.

88. Arminius, "Junius," 3:44; idem, "Perkins's," 3:342; Dell, "Man's Freedom," 146; Laytham, "Natural Theology," 35.

89. Witt, "Creation," 215.

The Views of Free Choice in the Postlapsarian State

Witt's summary about Arminius's concern, I do so with the understanding that Arminius's and Witt's understanding of Christocentrism differ from a traditional Reformed view of Christocentrism—Christ alone. For Arminius and Witt, Christocentric does not mean that Christ alone definitively accomplishes man's redemption. For them, Christocentric means that God's first decree in predestination was to choose Christ to be mediator, and that through his work as mediator Christ made it possible for man to choose to cooperate in the salvation process. And whatever else Arminius and Witt mean by Christocentric, it does not exclude man's cooperation unaided by special grace.

In order to protect God's immutable justice and goodness, Arminius maintains the free choice of the creature, so that his free choice wrongly employed serves as the grounds of his condemnation, and not the preordained will of God ipso facto. In this way, man is truly responsible for his sin(s).[90] Moreover, the teaching that some men are divinely determined to condemnation apart from their free choice in the matter would mean that some men are beyond redemption—an unacceptable thought for Arminius.[91] For Arminius, this impugns the goodness and justice of God. Therefore, Arminius believes that man possesses free choice to reject or accept efficacious grace, to do good, and to cooperate in the salvation process. In addition, Arminius continues to maintain an intellectualist position in the fallen state.

Were we simply to take Arminius's apparently clearer statements on the matter, we too would agree with Bangs and Hoenderdaal, who have concluded that Arminius believes man does not possess free choice in his fallen state. In one of his disputations, he seems to inveigh against the notion that man has free choice in his fallen state. He says, for example,

> In this [fallen] state, the free will of man [*liberum hominis arbitrium*] towards the True Good is not only wounded, maimed, infirm, bent, and weakened; but it is also imprisoned, destroyed, and lost: And its powers are not only debilitated and useless unless they are assisted by grace, but it has no powers whatever except such as are excited by Divine grace: For Christ has said, "Without me ye can do nothing."[92]

Granted, in the above quote Arminius is not yet talking about choosing to do the good but about the inclination to good and the true good. However,

---

90. Dell, "Man's Freedom," 157.

91. Ibid., 190. A little humanism creeps in at this point, since it appears that Arminius now becomes the judge of what is and is not acceptable.

92. Arminius, "Public," 2:192; idem, *Opera Theologica*, 211.

the implications are significant, since inclination and choice are the two departments of the faculty of will (*voluntas*).[93] Furthermore, he continues speaking of man being "dead in sin," with the resulting consequence that "our will is not free from the first fall; that is, it is not free to good, unless it be made free by the Son through his Spirit."[94]

In another place, when introducing his treatment of Romans 7, he tells of those being accused of the "twofold heresy of Pelagius," including himself, who believe Paul speaks of a man living under the law in an unregenerate state.[95] After naming the twofold heresy of Pelagius as ascribing "to man, without the grace of Christ, some true and saving good, and" maintaining that the regenerate can attain "a perfection of righteousness in the present life," Arminius vehemently rejects this conclusion, saying, "But I ingenuously confess, that I detest from my heart the consequences which are here deduced."[96] Thus, included in this teaching of Pelagius, which is rejected and detested by Arminius, is the assertion that man can do some true and saving good.

These statements presented above against free choice and against man's ability to do good seem to be in accord with the teaching of the Reformation as Calvin would have presented it, but only if we forget about the important qualifiers—"unless they are assisted by grace," "unless it be made free by the Son through his Spirit," and "without the grace of Christ"—and the meaning Arminius ascribes to these qualifiers.[97] Perhaps, more importantly, we ought not to forget Arminius's view of the nature of God and his relation to human beings as created. Therefore, before I address the qualifiers just mentioned and the issue of being inclined to do good and actually doing good, let us turn to Arminius's view of what happened to the *imago Dei* in the fall. Previously, I have pointed out that man's union with God took place initially by virtue of God creating man in his own image, which included endowing man with the faculties of understanding, will, and free choice itself. Since God is a being who possesses free choice as part of his nature, man as created in God's image

---

93. Hoitenga, *John Calvin*, 25, 29, 55; Calvin, *Sermons on Deuteronomy*, 1016.

94. Arminius, "Public," 2:194; idem, *Opera Theologica*, 212: "fequiter arbitrium nostrum à lapsu primo liberum non esse, ad bonum nempe, nisi à Filio per Spiritum ipsius liberetur."

95. Arminius, "Romans," 2:489–90.

96. Ibid., 2:489–90.

97. We will return to these qualifiers below.

necessarily has free choice as an essential part of his nature. Otherwise man would not be a true image bearer of God.

But what happened to the free choice that God gave to man at creation in light of the fall? Free choice is still present. After presenting the essential constitutive parts of the image of God in man, Arminius writes, "For that image of God which is essential to man, or that part which belongs to man's essence, remains in him even after sin."[98] Then, while discussing the providence of God, following the Thomistic tradition, Arminius says the foundation of permission (a significant concept in Arminius's teaching, where God in his governance permits man to sin but does not decree the fall and the subsequent sins of man) is "the freedom to choose, with which God formed his rational creature, and which his *constancy does not suffer to be abolished*, lest He should be accused of mutability."[99] In another place, he argues that he approves of anyone who "ascribes as much as possible to Divine Grace; provided he so pleads the cause of grace, as not to inflict an injury *on the Justice of God*, and *not to take away the free choice* to that which is evil."[100] Though Arminius mentions a free choice to do evil here, as we will see, he does not therefore exclude free choice to do good in the fallen state.

For Arminius, it is contrary to the divinely created order and his immutable justice for God to take away the ability of man to exercise his free choice. For God to have done so, he would have been denying himself and vitiating the integrity of man as a being created in the image of God. Therefore, even after the fall, man's integrity as a creature with free choice is upheld. The issue here is not whether man has *voluntas* (a will) but whether he has *arbitrium* (the ability to choose). All agree that *voluntas*, as a faculty of the soul, was not destroyed due to the fall and still remains uncoerced.[101]

---

98. Arminius, "Junius," 3:118. Olson fails to take this aspect of Arminius's teaching into consideration.

99. Arminius, "Public," 2:167 (emphasis added); idem, *Opera Theologica*, 200: "*est tum libertas arbitrii, cum qua creaturam rationalem condidit Deus, quam Constantia ipsius rescindi non patitur, ne mutabilitatis infimuletur Deus.*" Note Arminius's strong defense of the traditional doctrine of God's immutability, contra Pinnock and Boyd; see also Arminius, "Oration III," 1:377. John Patrick Donnelly argues that prominent Calvinists such as Peter Martyr Vermigli and Jerome Zanchi were Thomists on many points, including this matter of free will after the fall, contrary to "Calvin's strictures" (Donnelly, "Calvinist Thomism," 445, 451).

100. Arminius, "Hippolytus," 2:700–701 (emphasis added); idem, *Opera Theologica*, 772: "*qui gratiae agat, ne iustitiae Dei noxam inferat, & ne liberum arbitrium ad malum tollat.*"

101. Arminius, "Junius," 3:118.

Arminius's doctrine of creation regulates and dictates his understanding of the state and function of the will in a postlapsarian situation. Though I am not drawing this conclusion, one could make a case that man possesses free will by virtue of creation alone and apart from supernatural grace.

Nevertheless, we must now ask, what then is the nature of the freedom that man possesses in his fallen state according to Arminius? I will limit the discussion to considering the ability of man to do spiritual or saving good and evil, the question of synergism in salvation, and the question of the priority of the will or intellect. In limiting the discussion this way, I will exclude any significant discussion of the issues of Arminius's view and use of "Middle Knowledge" as it relates to God's foreknowledge and human contingencies.[102]

Concerning the issue of whether man is able to do saving good in his fallen state, again, if we take some statements of Arminius in isolation from everything else, we may be led to believe that he holds to the view that man can do no true spiritual good in his fallen state. For example, he forthrightly declares that man,

> in his lapsed and sinful state . . . is not capable, of and by himself, either to think, to will, or to do that which is really good; but it is necessary for him to be regenerated and renewed in his intellect, affections or will, and in all his powers by God in Christ through the Holy Spirit, that he may be qualified rightly to understand, esteem, consider, will and perform whatever is truly good.[103]

Arminius continues, "But if our brethren really think, that man can do some portion of good by the powers of nature, they are themselves not far from Pelagianism." However, a few lines later he says, "If they believe, that 'a man, who is a stranger to the true knowledge of God,' *is capable of doing nothing good*, this ought in the first place to have been charged with heresy."[104] Thus, in a few sentences Arminius seems to be affirming that man both cannot and can do some good. However, he clinches the matter and leaves no ambiguity about what he is arguing for when, at the end of this apology, he writes that, according to the Scholastic divines,

---

102. For discussions of these matters, see Arminius, "Public," 2:123–24; Bryant, "Molina, Arminius," 93–103; Dekker, "Was Arminius a Molinist?," 337–52; Craig, "Middle Knowledge," 141–63; Crabtree, "Does Middle Knowledge Solve," 429–57; Helm, "Philosophical Issue," 485–97; Witt, "Creation," 316–70; Muller, "Gambit," 263–69; Muller, "God, Predestination," 442–44; and MacGregor, *Luis de Molina*.

103. Arminius, "Declaration," 1:659–60.

104. Arminius, "Apology," 2:15 (emphasis added).

'God will do that which is in him, for the man who does what is in himself.' But, even then, the explanation of the Schoolmen ought to have been added—'that God will do this, not from [the merit of] condignity, but from [that of] congruity; and not because the act of man merits any such thing, but because it is befitting the great mercy and beneficence of God.' Yet this saying of the Schoolmen I should myself refuse to employ, except with the addition of these words: 'God will bestow more grace upon that man who does what is in him by the power of Divine Grace which is already granted to him according to the declaration of Christ, *To him that hath shall be given* [Matt 13:11–12].[105]

The assumption here is that man does some good—by divine grace—in order to receive more grace from God. The person doing the good by divine grace is, at this point, an unregenerate and unconverted person. It is clear then that, in Arminius's view, man in his fallen state is capable of doing good. In one of his apologies he again says, "We constantly assert, no good action whatever can be produced by man." However, further in the paragraph, he tells us what he really means. He believes man can do no good *without primary grace*.[106] In his comments on Romans 7, Arminius says, "*To will [velle] that which is good* [in the sense of outward conformity to the law], which is here the subject of the apostle's argument, is not peculiar to the regenerate; for it also *appertains to the unregenerate*."[107] Is he, however, working with a distinction between earthly and heavenly good? If this were so, his view would share some affinity to that of Calvin. In addition to this outward and earthly good, however, Arminius further teaches that the grace of the Holy Spirit is also given to the unregenerate, enabling them to desire and to do good that is pleasing to God.[108]

In Arminius's thinking, the grace (albeit supernatural, à la Olson) sufficiently needed for man to exercise his free choice, to will and to do good is given to all men in creation (first union with God in legal theology) and in Christ (second union with God in evangelical theology). Though the fall has a serious debilitating and deleterious effect upon man as he was originally created, in Christ (in addition to his created integrity) a new creation takes place, enabling man to do true *spiritual good*. In one discussion, Arminius sets aside discussing whether man has the "free will [*liberi arbitrii*]

---

105. Ibid., 2:16.
106. Ibid., 2:19–20.
107. Arminius, "Romans," 2:538 (emphasis added); idem, *Opera Theologica*, 699.
108. Arminius, "Romans," 2:541–43, 632.

to understand, will, and do natural and animal good things," assuming that this is a given that does not need to be addressed.[109] He then immediately goes on to say,

> we will . . . enter on the consideration of *spiritual good*, that concerns the spiritual life of man, which he is bound to live according to godliness,—inquiring from the Scriptures what powers man possesses, while he is in the way of animal life, to understand, to will [*volendum*], and *to do spiritual good things, which alone are truly good and pleasing to God.*"[110]

In his comments on Romans 7, after citing various Scripture references, he, again setting forth his position, says, "From these passages it is evident, that it cannot be said with truth, that nothing of good can be attributed to the unregenerate."[111] And, as if rebutting those who would say these good things are not of a saving nature, Arminius responds that "they [good works] are themselves in a certain degree saving."[112] It is clear, then, that Arminius teaches that man can choose to do some saving and spiritual good that is pleasing to God in his fallen state.

In addition to the created inherent free choice that allows man to perform spiritual good, *grace* enables all men to use their free choice to do spiritual good. Here, I take up the qualifiers of "being assisted by grace," "being set free by the Spirit" and "by the power of divine grace," as I show that Arminius believes in free choice in the fallen state by looking at the question of synergism.

What does synergism mean? Louis Berkhof considers it "an act of man, co-operating with divine influences" to be worthy of the title "the synergistic theory of regeneration," which is "Semi-Pelagian and Arminian."[113] Olson, on the other hand, claims Arminius's synergism is not humanistic and is neither of the Pelagian nor semi-Pelagian stripe, but is an evangelical

---

109. Arminius, "Public," 2:191; idem, *Opera Theologica*, 211.

110. Arminius, "Public," 2:191 (emphasis added); idem, *Opera Theologica* (Leiden: 1629), 263. Note that this is a different edition of Arminius's *Opera Theologica* than the one I have used predominantly in this book. This edition is available in the Swedenborgian Library and Archives at the Pacific School of Religion, which is part of the Graduate Theological Union (GTU) catalogue, located in Berkeley, California. In order to distinguish this edition from the other edition, which is located at Calvin College and Seminary's Heckman Library, future references will be cited as *Theologica*.

111. Arminius, "Romans," 2:541.

112. Arminius, "Romans," 2:541.

113. Berkhof, *Systematic*, 473.

The Views of Free Choice in the Postlapsarian State

synergism, which he defines as "the prevenience of grace to every human exercise of a good will toward God, including simple nonresistance to the saving work of Christ."[114] Another authority defines synergism as "the doctrine of cooperation of human effort and divine regeneration."[115] Though attempting to soften the implication of the idea of cooperation with grace in the definition of synergism, even Karl Rahner and Herbert Vorgrimler acknowledge that "the magisterium of the Church freely speaks of man's 'co-operation' with grace" as essential to the definition of synergism.[116] For our purposes, then, I will take synergism to mean freely cooperating with grace in the process of salvation, whether or not co-earning is involved. Monergism would then be the absence of man's cooperation with grace in salvation, with or without the concept of co-earning. Bangs and Witt seem to be working with a less traditional understanding of the term.

When Arminius talks about grace, he does not work with the distinction between common and special grace, where the former has to do with the general benevolence of God to all men and the latter his special saving acts toward his elect. For Arminius, the operation of God's grace in man is universal, transcending all the states of man. Arminius would appeal Titus 2:11, "For the grace of God that brings salvation has appeared to all men," to support the universal presence of grace in all men. When extolling the free choice of man to do "the true good" prior to the fall, he writes, "Yet none of these acts could he do, *except through the assistance of Divine Grace.*"[117] Even with prevenient grace, God never denies concurrence to the acting creature.[118]

Moreover, when Arminius speaks of foreseen faith, he points out that the cause of faith is grace. He says, "Among those causes I consider the preventing, accompanying and succeeding [subsequent] grace of God."[119] For the person who has never read Arminius and has been taught that Arminius (as well as Arminians) denies the grace of God in man's salvation and attributes salvation to man's will alone, unaided by God's grace, these

---

114. Olson, *Arminian Theology*, 18.

115. Kawerau, "Synergism," 223; A similar definition of synergism is found in Elwell, ed., *Concise Evangelical Dictionary*, 494.

116. Rahner and Vorgrimler, "Synergism," 492.

117. Arminius, "Declaration," 1:659.

118. Witt, "Creation," 390–91. Prevenient grace is the grace that comes before, enabling man to, as it were, prepare for salvation.

119. Arminius, "Apology," 1:749; Arminius, "Hippolytus," 2:700.

statements about the inability of man to do any spiritual good apart from grace can be quite perplexing. Overcoming the perplexity begins when one realizes that these various graces of God of which Arminius speaks are different only in quantity and not in quality. They are all efficacious in their place and in a limited sense. For example, the initial (first/prevenient) grace that is given to all men only grants them the ability to exercise free choice. It does not effectively induce the chooser to choose good over bad or vice versa. To so induce choice would go beyond the purpose for which this grace is given, which is to simply make free choice possible. This grace, then, is efficacious in its place in light of the purpose for which it is given; it gives man free choice. Thus, concerning this prevenient grace, Arminius states that "God 'prevenes' sufficiently and efficaciously."[120] Though he distinguishes between sufficient and efficient grace, Arminius's usage differs from Calvin's understanding of the distinction when he says, "By efficacious grace is meant not that which is received of necessity and cannot be refused, but that which is certainly accepted and is rejected by no one to whom it is applied."[121] The distinction becomes a distinction without any qualitative difference. Sufficient grace becomes efficient based on the creature's positive response and continuance in the grace given. Unlike what we have seen with Calvin, where efficacious grace changes the will and compels a response, this efficacious grace of Arminius does not overpower man and force him to respond positively to the gospel. This grace is efficacious only to move men "by a sweet and gentle suasion."[122]

Consequently, if man rightly uses each measure of grace in its proper place, God will give more grace to make man able, but not necessarily willing, to respond to the overtures of the gospel. The prevenient grace gives man the ability, efficaciously, to say yes or no to the gospel. All men, without distinction, have this grace given to them so that they have it in their power to respond positively (or negatively) to the external and internal call of grace.[123] Should men respond positively to the internal and external overtures of God, that is *their* doing. Those who have not been called externally through the ordinary means of the preaching of the word may still have an opportunity to respond to the extraordinary internal call of the

---

120. Arminius, "Perkins's," 3:472.
121. Ibid., 3:450.
122. Ibid.
123. Arminius, "Apology," 2:20.

Holy Spirit, who is not bound by the ordinary means of the external call but is free to intervene as he sees fit.[124]

As Bangs argues, Arminius rejects Perkins's distinction between common and special grace while distinguishing between prevenient, saving, and subsequent grace in order to highlight the continuity of grace, and not the quality of it, as is the case with Perkins's distinction.[125] Sufficient or prevenient grace enables man to respond positively to the gospel but does not make him actually respond. Sufficient grace is given to all men by virtue of pre-fall creative activity, providence, and post-fall re-creative activity of God in Christ.[126] In the words of Witt, "All human beings are given sufficient grace by which they might exercise faith. . . . The purpose of sufficient grace is to free the will from bondage to sin so that it might exercise faith."[127]

This one sufficient and efficient grace is part of God's general providential care for his rational creatures. For Arminius, providence is God maintaining to some degree that which he has begun in the original creation, in spite of the fall.[128] Thus, for example, he says, "For, according to the decree of providence by which he gives grace sufficient for believing, the exhortation to faith and repentance is instituted."[129] Arminius defines providence, in part, as God's work of exercising care "over each of the creatures and their actions and passions, in a manner that is befitting himself and suitable for his creatures."[130] In Arminius's teaching, God's providence never violates or undermines the creature's created mode of contingent existence, which guarantees man's possession and use of his free choice.

Nevertheless, in addition to providence, supernatural grace is added so that man *can* believe; though there is no guarantee that he *will* believe. This grace entices but does not effectually cause salvation. As Arminius again puts it, "The Author of grace has determined not to force men by his grace to assent, but by a sweet and gentle suasion to move them; which

---

124. Ibid., 2:20–22.

125. Bangs, "Arminius and the Reformation," 169.

126. Arminius, "Perkins's," 3:315, 316; Arminius, "Junius," 3:168.

127. Witt, "Creation," 656.

128. Arminius, "Certain Articles," 2:714; Arminius, "Junius," 3:168, 179; see 133, 196, 230, 232. It is worthwhile to note that Arminius uses another distinction of grace in his treatment of providence: there is the grace of conservation, which relates to providence, and the grace of restoration, which relates to the regenerating work of Christ.

129. Arminius, "Perkins's," 3:317.

130. Arminius, "Private," 2:367; see idem, "Hippolytus," 2:696–98; and idem, "Certain Articles," 2:714.

motion not only does not take away the free consent [*liberum consensum*] of a free will [*liberi arbitrii*], *but even strengthens it*."[131] In addition, that God commands man to believe implies that man has the free choice to believe and can believe if he wants.[132]

If man possesses such freedom of choice, not only is the free-choice response of man necessary in salvation, but grace becomes resistible.[133] For grace—prevenient and sufficient—to succeed and become efficacious, man must play his part and give his consent. If he does not give his consent, grace does not overpower him. As Bangs renders it, "'flexible' free will can resist grace. . . . It always remains within the power of free will to reject grace bestowed, and to refuse subsequent grace; because grace is not an omnipotent action of God, which cannot be resisted by man's free will."[134] Why one person would give his consent and another refuse to give his consent is a question that is left unanswered. Since all have prevenient grace, there is nothing that prevents all from using their free choice to accept Christ as Savior and Lord.

However, since it is the case that all men have been given prevenient grace and have free choice, the elect do not receive a special internal call in distinction from the reprobate. The internal call of God, which Arminius does not consider to be soteriologically effectual, "is granted even to those who do not comply with the call."[135] He then adds,

> All unregenerate persons have freedom of choice, and a capability of resisting the Holy Spirit, of rejecting the proffered grace of God, . . . of refusing to accept the Gospel of grace, and of not opening to Him who knocks at the door of the heart; and these things they can actually do, without any difference of the Elect and of the Reprobate.[136]

---

131. Arminius, "Perkins's," 3:450 (emphasis added); idem, *Opera Theologica*, 594.

132. Arminius, "Gomarus," 3:611.

133. Arminius, "Declaration," 1:629.

134. Bangs, "Arminius and the Reformation," 168.

135. Arminius, "Certain Articles," 2:721.

136. Ibid., 2:721; idem, *Opera Theologica*, 783: "*Omnes irregeniti habent liberum arbitrium, & potentiam Spiritui Sancto resistendi, gratiam Dei oblatam repudiandi, . . . Euangelium gratiae repudiandi, ei qui cor pulsat non aperiendo, idque actu ipso possunt facere, citta discrimen ullum Electorum, & Reproborum.*" I take "unregenerate" here to mean unregenerate in both the sense of those who "felt no motion of the regenerating Spirit" and those who "feel those motions of the Holy Spirit" (Arminius, "Apology," 2:17).

This grace, which gives all persons the ability to reject or accept the gospel, is given to all in Christ.[137]

In this context, Arminius makes a distinction between the obtainment of redemption and the application of redemption (salvation). The obtainment of redemption, which makes man even more able to accept or resist the grace of God, is universal. However, its application—which is salvation—is limited to those who exercise their free choice and believe. Laytham sees this understanding of grace given to all in Christ as an outflow of Arminius's brand of Christocentrism, which allows for man's cooperation in salvation—a negative, in Laytham's mind—in contrast to Witt's positive appraisal of this Christocentrism.[138]

Before moving on to address the issues of intellectualism and voluntarism, it needs to be noted that the inevitable effect of Arminius's view of grace serves to undercut his more explicit statements about the bondage of the will and the need for the grace of Christ. First of all, if man retains his free choice by virtue of being created in God's image, can it be said in any real sense that man was ever totally depraved and in bondage to sin? Though Arminius desires to maintain and confess the biblical teaching that fallen man is in bondage to sin, the logic of his teaching about grace inexorably leads to the conclusion that man was never really in total bondage to sin, since he was always in possession of the supernatural grace needed to freely choose God. The bondage and depravity of sin then appears to be a theoretical and nominal fiction. At best, it was a bondage that was very, very brief—nothing more than a mere momentary eclipse.

Secondly, if man retains free choice by virtue of creation, then the particular redemptive grace of Christ, which is made available after the fall in order to excite the bound will to become free to choose, appears to be logically superfluous since the will already possesses created free choice, by virtue of being an image bearer of God, which cannot be removed but is providentially retained. Granted, Olson and other true Arminians would strenuously reject this conclusion as much as Calvin and true Calvinists strenuously deny the charge that God is the author of sin—the inevitable conclusion of the divine determinist view of Calvin, according to Arminius.

In Arminius's view of grace as it is obtained generally for all men, fallen and redeemed, grace primarily affects the mind of fallen man. Hence, Arminius's postlapsarian view of man's will stands firmly in the

---

137. Arminius, "Perkins's," 3:306–8, 325, 336, 337, 422, 425, 447.
138. Laytham, "Natural Theology," 30; Witt, "Creation," 215.

intellectualist tradition. When Arminius talks about the effect of sin upon the soul of man, he locates the primary effect upon the mind of man. He says, for example, "To this darkness of mind succeeds the perverseness of the affections and of the hearts."[139] Then, when addressing punishment for sin, he describes it in one sense as the taking away of grace "by blinding the mind and hardening the heart."[140] Here, sin primarily affects the mind.

Arminius's presentation of the doctrine of repentance also confirms his intellectualism. Here, the understanding takes precedence. Says he, "Repentance, penitence, or conversion is an act of the entire man, by which in his *Understanding* he disapproves of sin universally considered, *in his Affections* he hates it . . . and in the whole of his life avoids it."[141] In his treatment of Romans 7, he says, "The mind . . . persuades the will of man to do that which is holy, and just, and good, and to reject what is merely delectable."[142] It seems very clear to us, then, that in the fallen state Arminius holds to a priority of the intellect over the will.

Conclusion Concerning Postlapsarian State

It seems obvious that the arguments made on both sides concerning the postlapsarian state show that there can be no rapprochement between the theological systems of Arminianism and Calvinism without one position being abandoned by its adherents.[143] The differences not only emerge more clearly, they abound.

Nevertheless, note that Calvin and Arminius agree that the fall did not result in the destruction of man's will (*voluntas*). They also agree that the will that survives the fall is free from compulsion. However, since man's choice, according to Calvin, is bound by his nature, he would rather the title "free choice" not be used to designate freedom from compulsion, since the title is very easily misunderstood. The term "free will" (choice) is too exalted a title for the scanty measure of freedom of which it speaks.

Though there are these general areas of agreement, Calvin and Arminius differ on the powers that remain in the corrupt will as it exists in the

---

139. Arminius, "Public," 2:193.
140. Ibid., 2:175.
141. Ibid., 2:237, 238; cf. 236.
142. Arminius, "Romans," 2:583.
143. Olson makes the point that the systems are so incompatible that there can't even be a hybrid of the two; Olson, *Arminian*, 61–77.

The Views of Free Choice in the Postlapsarian State

fallen state (post-lapse). The major difference between Calvin and Arminius at this point revolves around the radical nature of the fall.

Calvin's views on the nature and function of the will in the postlapsarian state are very different and contrary to Arminius's teaching on almost all points. That which remains of the created nature, for Calvin, is only the mere apparatus, devoid of its proper function. The *imago Dei* is so damaged by the fall that what is left is hardly recognizable. Hence, for Calvin, the will that persists after the fall is so deformed that it is devoid of free choice and is wholly inclined to evil. Arminius, on the other hand, holds that free choice is an essential attribute of man, which could not be taken away without making God mutable and the author of sin.[144] Calvin does not believe free choice is an essential attribute whose loss impinges upon the immutability of God and makes him the author of sin.

Though Hoitenga finds here an inconsistency in Calvin, I believe that there is a remarkable consistency in Calvin at this point in light of his own methodology. The fall is so radical that it requires the radical work of grace to restore a measure of free choice that was lost in the fall. Calvin is not interested in philosophical consistency—at least not the kind for which Hoitenga is looking. Calvin is consistent in letting the revealed word of God be his guide. Thus, he is willing to go in whatever direction the revealed word takes him, even if that direction appears logically inconsistent. I also disagree with Brümmer, who states Calvin taught that "free choice belongs to our nature and cannot be taken away from us by the fall."[145] This is what Arminius teaches and it plainly contradicts Calvin's clear teaching on the matter.

When it comes to deflecting the charge that God is the author of sin and to rendering man inexcusable before God, in the fallen state, Calvin does not adduce free choice for these purposes in the postlapsarian state. It is enough for Calvin that man was originally given free choice in the prelapsarian state. In addition to original free choice, that every created thing bears the imprint of God and testifies of him provides sufficient reason to render man inexcusable before God. Therefore, though free choice is absent in Calvin's postlapsarian state, man is still responsible before God; and he has no excuse for disobeying the commands of God. Nevertheless, though God commands obedience, Calvin maintains, contra Arminius, that man is unable to obey those commands of his own free choice. God commands what he wills and gives that which he commands.

144. Arminius, "Junius," 3:80–85, 208.
145. Brümmer, "Calvin, Bernard," 449.

Rather than adducing free choice, Calvin primarily espouses the bondage of the will. The limited freedom that Calvin attributes to the fallen will is, to use Hoitenga's language, the minimalist freedom from compulsion. This little freedom guarantees the voluntary nature of man's necessarily sinful activities. Nevertheless, Calvin argues strongly that man is a voluntary slave to sin.

Hence, the suggestion of Schreiner, Lane, and Brümmer that Calvin gives more or less lenient treatment to free choice, depending on whom his opponents are, needs slight modification at this point.[146] For in a passage where Calvin deals with the determinism of Stoics, he avers, "Hence we maintain that, by providence, not heaven and earth and inanimate creatures only, but also the counsels and wills of men are so governed as to move exactly in the course which he has destined."[147] Here, one would think Calvin would offer a more lenient treatment since he is addressing determinists; yet he does not. Witt is also not entirely fair then when, in light of his purpose for making the succeeding statement, he writes, "For Calvin, creation and providence are inextricably connected." Though there is a very logical (and yes, inextricable) connection in Calvin between creation and providence, nonetheless, creation and providence are more inextricably connected in Arminius's theology than that of Calvin's when one considers that primary purpose of providence in Arminius's thinking is to maintain intact certain essential aspects of man's created nature despite the fall. Witt is also not entirely correct when he argues from Calvin's view of providence that Calvin is a determinist, if determinism is understood in a philosophical/Stoic sense.[148]

Naturally, then, since man's will is so bound by sin and inclined to evil, it follows that, unlike Arminius, Calvin's fallen man can do no spiritual good. Contrary to Arminius and his supporter Witt, fallen man does not desire the supreme good of union and communion with God. For Calvin, though there is not a person who would not be satisfied with eternal blessedness, no one desires this blessedness apart from special grace. Witt is correct, therefore, when he notes that on this matter Calvin is at odds with the Thomist tradition;[149] whatever apparently good desires man has result from selfish ambition.

---

146. Schreiner, *Theater*, 16–19; Lane, "Did Calvin?," 74, 86; Brümmer, "Calvin, Bernard," 437.

147. Calvin, *Institutes*, I.xvi.8.

148. Witt, "Creation," 84, 85, 86, 89, 104.

149. Ibid., 96.

The Views of Free Choice in the Postlapsarian State

Since man neither can desire nor do spiritual good, the complete work of regeneration belongs, from start to finish, to God. Unlike the Arminian system, man is not prevened so that he is only enabled (but not made) to respond to a measure of grace already given. Thus, though for Arminius a beggar has the power of general grace in himself to stretch out his hand and receive the gift offered or to resist doing so, in Calvin's understanding the ability to stretch out the hand and receive the gift offered is also a direct result of God's special grace—a grace that effectually induces the response. For Calvin, efficacious grace so effectually induces a response that it is impossible for man to resist the internal call of God and deny the workings of grace. Calvin does not deny that there is prevenient grace. However, for him, when it comes to the matter of salvation, that grace, even if it comes in smaller quantities, cannot be resisted. Again, contrary to Arminius's view, this saving grace is only given to the elect who will believe. On all accounts, when it comes to the salvation of men, Calvin is a monergist.

A question that is left still unanswered by Arminius is why, even with free choice, one person chooses to reject the call of God while another person chooses to respond positively to that call? Why, still, does man choose one way or the other?

Consistent with his monergism, Calvin is a functional voluntarist in his understanding of fallen man. Though Witt recognizes this view of Calvin, he designates Calvin as a voluntarist erroneously when he argues that Calvin was simply following Scotus, who had affirmed that God, who is ruled by will, "does not need direction in his actions."[150] But Calvin is simply dealing with scriptural revelation and the radical reality of sin in the fallen state. George Harper's response to Kendall is both sufficient and efficient to dismiss the claim of Witt. Harper points out there are two voluntarist traditions: the older Scholastic tradition and the *via moderna* tradition.[151] Calvin inherited the older Scholastic tradition, which was Augustinian. The other tradition descended from Scotus.

Though Calvin's voluntarism may be logically inconsistent in light of his prelapsarian intellectualism, à la Hoitenga,[152] it appears that the kind of consistency Hoitenga is looking for is precluded when Calvin's authorial intentions are kept in mind.[153] I believe Laytham's suggestion that Calvin

---

150. Ibid., 12–13, 19–20, 28, 83.
151. Harper, "Calvin and English Calvinism," 259; see Muller, "Priority," 71.
152. Hoitenga, *John Calvin*, 48.
153. Armstrong, "*Duplex*," 136.

works with a whole series of biblical ideas that are not easy to reconcile logically is sufficient to remove the bite from Hoitenga's assertion.[154] Calvin's voluntarism stands in marked contrast to the thoroughgoing intellectualism of Arminius.

After Calvin presents the position of the philosophers on the soul and its divisions, Calvin rejects the view of the philosophers because they were not familiar with the corruption of nature.[155] Calvin would have said the same thing concerning Arminius's view of man's will. Granted, as Olson and others point out, Arminius does use language that underscores a radical corruption of man in his fallen state. But the logic of his arguments seems to undermine what he underscores with plain language.

The will that persists in the fallen state, for Arminius, is a will that has as part of its nature the power to exercise free choice. To Arminius, free choice is part of the apparatus created in us by God, who unites himself with us in such a way that if free choice did not persist, one would have to conclude that God is mutable, since this kind of "radical" change in the substance of the creature would necessarily mean that there is mutability in God, and/or that we are not true image bearers of God. Note here that, unlike modern open theists, Arminius has a strong view of God's immutability.

In addition, man retains his free choice after the fall because of providence (which preserves created contingency), general grace, and redemptive grace in Christ (which is obtained for all men). Hicks, therefore, is correct when he interprets Arminius to mean that unregenerate man retains freedom of choice as one of his essential attributes (by virtue of being created in the image of God, and apart from redemptive grace in Christ). However, he is incorrect when he claims that Arminius did not teach the free choice to do good or evil.[156]

In addition to preserving God's immutability, by positing free choice in fallen man, Arminius is also defending God against the charge of being the author of sin and vindicating his justice and goodness. If man does not have free choice, in Arminius's opinion, it would be unjust for God to punish man for sins he cannot help but commit. This would be nothing short of a cruel joke that God plays upon man bound to sin. Arminius, therefore, retains free choice in order to render man inexcusable before God. Arminius is looking at man individualistically and not federally à la Romans 5. If

---

154. Laytham, "Natural Theology," 23–24.

155. Calvin, *Institutes*, II.xv.7.

156. Hicks, "Theology of Grace," 36–37.

The Views of Free Choice in the Postlapsarian State

man does not have free choice, he must be determined. If he is determined, God is the cause of each man's continued sin and rebellion. Without free choice, man cannot help but sin. Without free choice, man also has an excuse and can say that he sins by compulsion due to a divine determinative decree. If God is the cause, man has an excuse before God—an excuse that would make it unjust for God to punish man for violating commands he could not keep. For Arminius, the command to obey implies the natural ability to obey. This ability that belongs to man by virtue of his free choice ensures that all the responsibility for sin rests squarely upon the shoulders of man alone and not upon God.

Moreover, with his free choice, man is able to do true spiritual good. The good that man can do in his fallen state, according to Arminius, is more than Hicks's metaphysical goodness.[157] I also disagree with Hicks's assessment that man, in Arminius's understanding, is only free to sin. Ultimately, in Arminius's thinking, man has it in his power to cooperate in the process of regeneration. Grace makes man able but not necessarily willing to respond to the external and internal call. Thus, Bangs is correct when he interprets Arminius to teach that "Grace rescues free will, but not without the choice of the will thus rescued."[158] I would also concur with Bangs's assessment that "all response of man to the divine vocation is the work of grace."[159] Witt would also agree with Bangs. Keep in mind, however, that this grace is not unique since it is given to every human being. The response of man to the call of God is not the work of any special grace but the work of man's will enabled by general grace. In Arminius's beggar illustration, the giver and grace certainly have the principal part to play, but man, however so slightly, does play a part by reaching out with his own general grace enabled strength to receive the gift.[160] Moreover, in this illustration, Arminius claims that "the beggar is always prepared to receive." This is synergism. How so? It is so because the level of grace given, which recuses free choice and makes man able to respond to the call of God, does not effectually cause salvation. In order for salvation to occur, more grace has to be given, without which man cannot be saved. Though there is no difference in the quality of grace, for man to be saved, he must act of his own will with the meager amounts of grace already given in order to receive the right quantity

---

157. Ibid., 37.
158. Bangs, *Arminius*, 216.
159. Ibid., 341.
160. Arminius, "Apology," 2:52.

that is necessary for salvation. Therefore, as Muller shows, this modified acceptance by Arminius of "the late medieval dictum, *facere quod in se est, Dues non denegat gratiam*," makes him a synergist.[161]

On the other side of this equation, not only does man have the free choice to cooperate positively with grace already given, Arminius teaches that man has the power to resist the internal call and the limited quantity of grace of God that is operative in all men.

Since the result of Arminius's God-centered theology is that he has a higher view of human will and its function in the fallen state, one would expect that he would espouse voluntarism. However, on the contrary, I find him to be a staunch intellectualist. Though the will sins, it does so under the guise of seeking the good. There is a natural inclination in man toward goodness. However, since the mind is darkened, it presents wrong choices to the will as good choices.

---

161. Muller, "Federal Motif," 107; cf. 122. The modification of Arminius reads, "God will bestow more grace upon that man who does what is in him by the power of Divine Grace which is already granted to him, according to the declaration of Christ, To him that hath shall be given . . . (Matt. xiii, 11, 12)" (Arminius, "Apology," 2:16). Arminius's specific addition is that part of the above quotation, which begins, "by the power . . ." Arminius's improvement is that he puts grace at the start of man's response, which enables him to do what in him lies. For further analysis of Arminius's acceptance of this medieval dictum and his use of the beggar illustration, see Fesko, "Arminius on *Facientibus Quod in se Est*," 347–60.

Chapter 3

The Views of Free Choice in the Redeemed State

Calvin: Man's Choice Is Primarily Free

IN THE PREVIOUS POSTLAPSARIAN state, Calvin primarily champions the bondage of human choice in matters of belief. The fall into sin had destroyed man's free choice. Now, however, in this redeemed state, special grace radically affects man's will for the good, with effects that match and supersede the radical effects of the fall. So radical is the effect of grace that the "habit"[1] of the will is transformed from being a slave to sin to being a servant of righteousness. Hence, in this redeemed state, man possesses freedom of choice.

There is less discussion in the literature with respect to Calvin's view of the will in the redeemed state. Some authors support the view that Calvin believes man possesses free choice in his redeemed state, as they acknowledge Calvin teaches that grace does not destroy but renews or repairs the will.[2] Lane states, however, that Calvin is liable to bear some blame for giving the impression that grace destroys the will.[3] Brümmer, on the other hand, maintains that though Calvin holds to free choice before the fall, he later advocates a view of grace that in effect destroys free will. Brümmer considers this switch a moment of inconsistency in Calvin.[4] Witt, agreeing with Brümmer, comments, "Calvin's understanding of regeneration

---

1. "Habit" is used in a medieval sense, where it refers to a "modification of the substance [as opposed to accidents] not so easily changed" (Lane, *Student*, 184).
2. Leith, "Doctrine," 56; idem, "Did Calvin?," 81–82; Schreiner, *Theater*, 102.
3. Lane, "Did Calvin?," 82.
4. Brümmer, "Calvin, Bernard," 452–55.

conflicts with the Thomist dictum that grace perfects nature rather than supplanting it," as he asserts that Calvin teaches that in regeneration God gives a new (i.e., different) will.[5]

With respect to priority of faculty, based on Calvin's inclusion of knowledge in his definition of faith, Kendall claims that Calvin is really an intellectualist.[6] Muller, on the other hand, argues that Calvin leans more in the direction of soteriological voluntarism since Calvin's use of knowledge in his definition of faith does not exclude the involvement of the will in faith.[7] In fact, there can be no true faith apart from the involvement of the will.[8]

The view that a particular theologian espouses concerning Calvin's view of free choice affects his interpretation of Calvin's view of perseverance of the saints. Thus, Brümmer holds that Calvin taught perseverance of the saints.[9] Larry Sharp, on the other hand, would have us believe that Calvin does not believe in perseverance of the saints. Sharp cites *Institutes*, III.xxiv.6 in support of his claim that Calvin teaches that some believers fall away and lose their salvation.[10] On the contrary, Calvin teaches that perseverance must be included with both faith and calling in order to claim the security of election. He then goes on to give ample biblical proofs supporting the truth that genuine believers in Christ will persevere to the end.

When Calvin discusses man in the redeemed state, it is usually against the background of what he had been in creation and became in the fall. Calvin sees a connection between the creation of man in the image of God and his re-creation in Christ. Commenting on 1 Corinthians 15:45, Calvin speaks of the end of regeneration as entailing the formation anew of God's people in the image of God. In regeneration, then, "The new man is renewed after the image of him that created him (Colossians 3:19, [*sic*; v. 10 is intended])."[11] For Calvin, a recovery of what was lost does take place in regeneration. In conjunction with Ephesians 4:24, Calvin sees this recovery of what was lost to have more specific reference to the divine gifts of knowledge, righteousness,

---

5. Witt, "Creation," 97.
6. Kendall, *Calvin and English*, 19.
7. Muller, "*Fides* and *Cognitio*," 217, 223.
8. Ibid., 221.
9. Brümmer, "Calvin, Bernard," 452.
10. Sharp, "Doctrines of Grace," 93. Apparently, Sharp only read the first half of that section, for in the second half Calvin goes on to argue the very opposite of Sharp's claim.
11. Calvin, *Institutes*, I.xv.4; see III.iii.9; III.xvii.5; II.ii.12; III.iii.9; and III.xvii.5.

and holiness. The paradise lost in the fall is partly regained in redemption. In this sense, effectual grace restores free choice.

But how well recovered is man's free choice? Is he now able to choose between good and evil to the same degree he was able to before the fall? Can man, with a restored free choice, obey the law, perfectly or imperfectly, with sincerity? Does man now possess the possibility of sinning? As Calvin begins to shed light on the answers to these questions, he states that redeemed man receives an upright will through the regenerating work of the Holy Spirit. But what does it mean to have an upright will? Calvin goes on to clarify, saying, "The Spirit does not confer on us the faculty of willing [*facultatem volendi*]: for it is inherent to us from our birth, that is, it is hereditary, and a part of the creation which could not be blotted out by Adam's fall; but when the will [*voluntas*] is in us, God gives us to will rightly [*recte velle*], and this is his work."[12] Calvin makes two points here. First, he again affirms that the faculty of will was never destroyed in the fall.[13] Second, in Calvin's understanding, willing rightly has to do with willing insofar as it relates to salvific belief in God. The ability to will rightly in this sense results from the supernatural efficacious gift of special grace. It is in this sense of willing rightly, then, that Calvin teaches that man has free choice in the redeemed state.

Redeemed man is now free to choose well with regard to spiritual matters. As we have seen, for Calvin, the unregenerate man is incapable of doing anything good and upright in the soteric sense. Unregenerate man is in bondage to sin with respect to spiritual matters. Thus, in regeneration, elect believers are released from their bondage to sin and given a new will through the special grace of God. Calvin clarifies that what he means by "new will" is a new disposition of the will. The old will (*voluntas*) is now renewed with the power of choice (*arbitrium*). The change is so radical that it is *as if* man was given a new faculty for willing. Calvin speaks of the change that takes place in the will according to the biblical metaphor of turning a heart of stone into one of flesh. He writes,

> God turns us to the study of rectitude, everything proper to our own will [*voluntatis*] is abolished, and that which succeeds in its place is wholly of God. I say the will [*voluntatem*] is abolished, but not in so far as it is will [*voluntas*], for in conversion everything essential to our original nature remains: I also say, that it is created

---

12. Calvin, *Ezekiel*, 11:379; *Calvini, Opera Omnia*, 40:248.
13. Calvin, *Institutes*, II.iii.14; II.v.15.

anew, not because the will [*voluntas*] then begins to exist, but because it is turned from evil to good.[14]

When, therefore, man receives the new (disposition of) will through the special grace of God, he is primarily free to do good, to seek after God and the things of God.

For Calvin, the grace given to redeemed man that makes him choose spiritual good is qualitatively different from the grace of creation and providence. Only the elect receive the special grace that causes them to choose to will and do spiritual good. In his comments on parts of Romans 7, Calvin says, "This applies to none but the regenerate, who, with the leading powers of the soul, tend toward what is good."[15] Again he writes, "It is certainly easy to prove that the commencement of good is only with God, and that none but the elect have a will [*voluntas*] inclined to good."[16] As we will see in a moment, all this does not mean that the redeemed man always chooses to do what is spiritually good. However, with this special and redeeming grace, man now knows the good as good and has the power to choose that good.

When Calvin talks about doing good, he has in mind salvific or heavenly good, as opposed to various manifestations of general providence in the lives of sinners who do many good and noble things according to purely earthly standards.[17] An unregenerate person can be an excellent surgeon, for example. This is an earthly good that has no spiritual and eternal saving benefit. However, this excellent unregenerate surgeon can choose to do no spiritual good except through the gift of special, redeeming grace. Only the redeemed person has the freedom of choice to choose to do saving and spiritual good. Now, that the redeemed man has the free choice to do good does not mean that he now cooperates with God and contributes something to his salvation. Calvin means that only regenerate people, who have the special indwelling of the Spirit of God, are able to aspire to "eternal blessedness."[18] The primary aspect of freedom of choice that man receives in the redeemed state is the freedom to do spiritual good—a quality that was lost in the fall.

---

14. Ibid., II.iii.6; *Calvini, Opera Omnia*, 2:215.

15. Calvin, *Institutes*, II.ii.27. Contra Arminius, Calvin believes the person described in Romans 7 is regenerate man.

16. Ibid., II.iii.8; *Calvini, Opera Omnia*, 2:217. See Calvin, *Institutes.*, II.iii.5, 6.

17. Calvin, *Institutes*, II.ii.13, 14, 15.

18. Ibid., II.ii.26; see II.ii.6.

The Views of Free Choice in the Redeemed State

The new ability to do spiritual good does not arise, however, merely out of a saved free choice that now acts on its own to aspire to and do spiritual good. The good that a regenerate person is able to do arises entirely out of the grace of God through the work of the Holy Spirit, who *moves* and *directs the will of man*. Calvin says,

> Hence it appears that the grace of God . . . is the rule of the Spirit, in directing and governing the human will [*voluntatem*]. Govern he cannot, without correcting, reforming, renovating. . . . In like manner, he cannot govern without moving, impelling, urging, and restraining. Accordingly, all the actions which are afterwards done are truly said to be wholly his [God's]. . . . There is nothing then to prevent us from saying, that our will [*voluntas*] does what the Spirit of God does in us, although the will contributes nothing of itself apart from grace. . . . Any intermixture which men attempt to make by conjoining the effort of their own free choice [*ex liberi arbitrii*] with divine grace is corruption. . . . But though every thing good in the will [*voluntate*] is entirely derived from the influence of the Spirit, yet, because we have naturally an innate power of willing [*velle*], we are not improperly said to do the things of which God claims for himself all the praise.[19]

However, though redeemed man is able to do spiritual good through the grace of God that captivates the will, because of the old nature in him, he is still able and liable to sin. In Calvin's interpretation, the individual mentioned in Romans 7 as a model still sins though he has a strong desire to do what is good. Though redeemed man is primarily free to do spiritual good, he is, however, still able to do evil. Calvin accepts the Augustinian position of *posse non peccare* (able not to sin) when he uses language such as, "we have a much greater freedom [than Adam]—viz. not to be able to sin."[20] Therefore, the redeemed person is not bound to sin. That person has the ability to exercise choice and not sin. However, Calvin is not a perfectionist who teaches that people can attain a level of sinlessness in this life in obedience to God. No! He accepts the other half of the Augustinian dictum, *posse peccare* (able to sin), which applies in the redeemed state as well. Calvin conveys his acceptance of this Augustinian principle when he says,

> The children of God are delivered from the bondage of sin, but not as if they had already obtained full possession of freedom

---

19. Ibid., II.v.15; idem, *Opera Omnia*, 2:243; see *Institutes*, II.iii.8.
20. Calvin, *Institutes*, II.iii.13; idem, *Bondage*, 241.

> [*libertatis*], and no longer felt any annoyance from the flesh. Materials for an unremitting contest remain, that they may be exercised, and not only exercised, but may better understand their weakness.[21]

In the end, the faithful are never so regenerated as to perfectly fulfill the law of God. Nevertheless, they strive to obey the laws of God with sincerity.[22]

Though individuals are unable to live a perfectly righteous life in this world, the work of grace so dominates the will that redeemed people can have certainty that they will persevere and never fall outside of the sphere of God's special and saving grace. Redeemed people do not have the free choice to remove themselves from under the saving grace of God. They may temporarily appear to be strangers to the kingdom of God. Nevertheless, they are ultimately unable to lose their salvation. Calvin points out that the sophist idea that there is a moment where everyone is free to obey or reject "is obviously excluded by the doctrine of effectual perseverance."[23]

In setting forth his doctrine of perseverance, Calvin allows for a mild distinction between operating and cooperating grace, with some qualifications. "If," says Calvin, "it is meant that after we are once subdued by the power of the Lord to the obedience of righteousness, we proceed voluntarily, and are inclined to follow the movement of grace, I have nothing to object." On the other hand, "If, again, it is meant that man is able of himself to be a fellow-labourer with the grace of God, I hold it to be the most pestilential delusion."[24]

In Calvin's view, then, just as there is a necessity in fallen man to sin, yet without compulsion, in a similar manner, redeemed man necessarily perseveres in the salvation God in Christ bestows upon him. Yet, this necessity of perseverance is devoid of all coercion. God, by his grace, makes the will willing. The will acts freely now, according to the new spiritual nature that has been given it.

Therefore, on the question of voluntarism versus intellectualism, Calvin continues to maintain the voluntaristic perspective in the redeemed state. He locates the commencement of conversion in the will.[25] Without repeating all that I have already presented, one cannot miss noting that,

---

21. Calvin, *Institutes*, III.iii.10; *Calvini, Opera Omnia*, 2:441; see *Institutes*, III.iii.14.
22. Calvin, *Ezekiel*, 11:381; see Calvin, *Institutes*, II.vii.5.
23. Calvin, *Institutes*, II.iii.10.
24. Ibid., II.iii.11.
25. Ibid., II.iii.6.

though not to the exclusion of the intellect, attention to man's will dominates the discussion of the redeemed state. The will is first converted and then the mind is. Man is given a new will in conversion.

In the end, Calvin succinctly summarizes his own position on the matters discussed thus far when he writes, "Thus simply to will is the part of man, to will ill the part of corrupt nature, to will well the part of grace."[26]

Arminius: Man's Choice Is More Free

If, as we have seen, man does not lose his free choice in his fallen state, perhaps the question we should ask at this juncture is: is there anything new in Arminius's understanding of the will? With the aid of grace, in the fallen state man has the power to accept or reject the gospel, to do or not to do good, and to cooperate or not cooperate with grace. Now, in the redeemed state, in answer to the question posed above, not much is new; however, matters relating to the will have just gotten better.

As we have seen with Calvin, much of the discussion in the literature recedes from this point on. However, Bangs tells us that for Arminius, "The regenerate man has free will. It is a free will neither of native endowment nor of good residue left over from the fall; rather it is the gift of grace, the gift of Jesus Christ."[27] Based on Arminius's own teaching of the creation of man in the image of God, though, it truly can be said that the free will in man stems from natural endowment, since it is part of what remains after the fall, in addition to being a gift of grace in Christ.

Pertaining to the question of the priority of the intellect or the will, Kendall argues that Arminius, in line with the "experimental predestinarians," falls into the voluntarist camp while Muller argues that Arminius belongs to the intellectualist camp.[28] Kendall argues that Arminius is a voluntarist because, due to his use of the word "approval," the will must be involved in the act of faith.[29] Contrary to Kendall, Muller argues that when Arminius uses "approval" he has in mind *assensus* (assent), which in Arminius's understanding is constitutive of functions of intellect and will—both of which are part of Arminius's grace gift from God.[30] Therefore, according to Muller,

---

26. Ibid., II.iii.5.
27. Bangs, *Arminius*, 191.
28. Muller, "Priority," 55–72; Kendall, *Calvin and English*, 19, 142–49.
29. Kendall, *Calvin and English*, 147.
30. Muller "Priority," 58–61.

in Arminius's soteriology, the traditional part of faith that involves the will—trust—is placed mainly outside of the definition of faith.[31]

In looking at Arminius's view of the will in the redeemed state, the pivotal place that the doctrine of creation plays in Arminius's system reasserts itself at this point. On this point, Muller shows that in Arminius's teaching "redemption itself is to be so understood as a re-creation of humanity that the doctrine of creation is a necessary presupposition of the doctrine of redemption."[32] This is not entirely illegitimate since paradise lost is paradise regained. In one of his responses to Gomarus's theses, Arminius takes issue with Gomarus's understanding of Paul's meaning when he speaks of the potter making one vessel for honor and one for dishonor in Romans 9. In setting forth his understanding of the matter, Arminius writes, "I say, then, that vessels to honor and of mercy are not made in the first [creation], but in the second and new creation." Then, after citing 2 Corinthians 5:17, which says, "If anyone be in Christ he is a new creation; behold old things have passed away and all things have become new," Arminius adds, "They were made such, not by generation [creation in the image of God at birth], but by regeneration [creation in Christ], and by the renewing of the Holy Ghost."[33] Thus, here in Arminius there is a creation and re-creation motif.

Arminius, in his conference with Junius, holds that the image of God constitutes two parts: the essential and the accidental. The accidental part includes knowledge of God, righteousness, and holiness (supernaturals). Concerning the essential part, which is made up of "soul, mind, affection, and will," Arminius teaches that in the redeemed state the essential part of the image is not "ingenerated or created in us, *for we have not lost it*; but to be restored and renewed in us, because it was deformed and corrupted."[34] He then adds, "Both therefore are true; for God's image is restored and renovated in us, namely, our mind and will, and the affections of soul: and God's image is ingenerated and increated in us, namely, the knowledge of God, righteousness and holiness of truth."[35] This at first may seems no different from the view of Calvin—where the naturals (*voluntas*) are not essentially created anew (since it was never destroyed) and the supernaturals (*arbitrium*), which were destroyed, are created anew. But we must

---

31. Ibid., 61–63.
32. Muller, "God, Predestination," 440.
33. Arminius, "Gomarus," 3:619.
34. Arminius, "Junius," 3:118 (emphasis added).
35. Ibid.

remember, for Arminius, what it means for man to have been created in the in the image of God. You will recall the teaching of Arminius that union with God and man began to take place at the time of creation when man was created in God's image. He made a distinction between the natural and supernatural aspects of the image. The soul, with its understanding (mind), affections, will, and free choice, makes up part of the natural aspect of the image of God, and knowledge, righteousness, and holiness make up the supernatural part of the image.[36] You will also remember that it is in the natural part that Arminius locates free choice. In addition, this "liberty of choosing [*libertas arbitrii*], with which God formed his rational creature... his constancy does not suffer to be abolished, lest He should be accused of mutability."[37] Herein lies one of the most significant differences between Calvin and Arminius, since for Calvin free will is located not in the natural part of man that persists after the fall but in the supernatural part that has been removed. However, the point here is to show that Arminius still holds to a measure of human free choice *via nature* in the redeemed state.

Arminius's view here harmonizes quite well with the Thomistic teaching that grace does not supplant nature but elevates and perfects it. Certainly, there is a sense in which Calvin agrees that grace perfects and elevates nature. However, it appears that for Aquinas and Arminius the grace that is added to nature in this redeemed state is good grace, but not a grace that is absolutely necessary for man. Moreover, the grace of which Aquinas and Arminius speak does not effect a radical change upon sinful man. To use Arvin Vos's words, in the teaching of Aquinas, "Grace both restores the supernatural gifts and heals the wounded nature."[38] Keep in mind that free choice is located in the wounded—not destroyed—nature, according to Arminius. It seems that for both Aquinas and Arminius, grace's primary function is to help sinful nature. For Calvin, grace is not only good; it is absolutely necessary and effects a change in man's sinful nature. Arminius, in his letter to a Collibus, asserts that the teacher who does not present grace in such a way that it takes away free choice (*liberum arbitrium*) will receive

---

36. Ibid., 3:95, 109–18, 153, 161, 439. Arminius will argue that in the fall the naturals were corrupted while the supernaturals were taken away.

37. Arminius, "Public," 2:167; idem, *Opera Theologica*, 201. See also idem, "Declaration," 1:659.

38. Vos, *Aquinas, Calvin*, 147; see also 14, 117, 120 136–38. Note that Vos argues that Aquinas has been misrepresented on this and others points. However, I believe Vos's arguments are unconvincing on this point.

his highest approval.[39] In another place he says, "For 'the Spirit which causes us actually to walk,' does not take away the liberty of man's will and choice [*libertatem arbitrii*]; but so acts in the free will [*libero arbitrio*] as He knows to be fitting and adapted for moving it certainly and infallibly."[40] For Arminius,

> Grace is so attempered and commingled with the nature of man, as not to destroy within him the liberty of his will [*libertatem voluntatis*], but give it a right direction, to correct its depravity, and to allow man to possess his own proper motions: While . . . this predestination introduces such species of grace, as takes away free will [*liberum arbitrium*] and hinders its exercise.[41]

We ought not to miss, however, that the thrust of Arminius's arguments thus far is to protect free choice, which is *already present* in fallen man from the time of creation, against the grace of predestination (and any other grace), which would destroy that free choice.

Another aspect of the creation and re-creation motif that figures prominently in the discussion at this point is the concept of union with God. As we have seen, the process of union with God, which began at creation, was never completed, due to natural limitations, and was severely interrupted by the fall of man into sin. Therefore, though the union was not severed, there was a significant setback toward this union. Nevertheless, now that God has become man in Christ, those who are united in Christ experience union with God in a way they never experienced before. Redeemed man now experiences union with God insofar as he is united with Christ, who is the very image of God.[42] Through this new union, man is well on the way to becoming what he could have been and should have been. He is well on the way to realizing his full created potential.

In one of his orations, Arminius tells us that what happens in natural/legal theology, which has to do with man in the created state of innocence, is only "a commencement of divine intercourse with him [man]." In this same paragraph, he contrasts what was begun in creation to the manifestation of the gospel (evangelical theology), and says, "God appears to have excelled himself, and to have unfolded every one of his blessings." He continues, "Admirable was the kindness of God, and most stupendous his condescension

---

39. Arminius, "Hippolytus," 2:700; idem, *Opera Theologica*, 772.
40. Arminius, "Perkins's," 3:474; idem, *Opera Theologica*, 606.
41. Arminius, "Declaration," 1:628–29; idem, *Opera Theologica*, 87.
42. Arminius, "Oration II," 1:367–70.

The Views of Free Choice in the Redeemed State

in admitting man to the most intimate communion with himself."[43] As Witt latter puts it, "The image of God in which human being was originally created thus anticipates the restored image of God recreated in Christ."[44]

It is only natural, in light of what we have been saying, that since God possesses free choice, the creature who is united with him in Christ continues to possess free choice in the redeemed state. However, no longer does the creature just have free choice as such; to use Bangs's language, "it is free will that is saved" and continues to concur with subsequent grace in the maintaining of the redemption already accomplished and presently being applied.[45]

If free choice is restored to a "saved" status in the redeemed state, then it naturally follows that on earth redeemed man can perform true spiritual good like never before. Redeemed man has far more freedom to choose. Arminius says, for example, "When he is made a partaker of this regeneration or renovation, I consider that, since he is delivered from sin, he is capable of thinking, willing [*velle*], and doing that which is good, but yet *not without the continued aids of Divine Grace*."[46] For Arminius, the grace of God at the point of union is an infusion of the gifts that pertain to regeneration. These gifts of faith, hope, and charity enable man to know and will the good.[47] With these gifts, the redeemed man more positively "loves and embraces that which is good, just, and holy;—and that, being made . . . capable in Christ, co-operating now with God he prosecutes the Good which he knows and loves, and he begins himself to perform it in deed."[48]

Arminius is so clear on this matter of man's free choice to do good in the redeemed state that he was accused of holding to a doctrine of perfectionism—the teaching that the redeemed person is able to live a life of sinlessness in this world. In his defense against this accusation, he neither denies nor affirms that redeemed man can live perfectly without sin in this life. The most he affirms, while appealing to the authority of Augustine, is that "they could do this [perfectly keep the law] by the grace of Christ, and by no means

---

43. ibid, 1:360.
44. Witt, "Creation" 466.
45. Bangs, "Arminius and Reformed," 118. Arminius himself says, "Take away free will [*liberum arbitrium*], and nothing will be left to be saved" (Arminius, "Public," 2:196; idem, *Opera Theologica*, 213).
46. Arminius, "Declaration," 1:660; idem, *Theologica*, 122.
47. Arminius, "Declaration," 1:664.
48. Arminius, "Public," 2:194–95.

without it."⁴⁹ He also states, "The regenerate are able to perform *more* true good, and of such as is pleasing to God, than they actually perform, and to omit more evil than they omit."⁵⁰ A few lines later he adds, "He who asserts that 'it is possible for the regenerate, through the grace of Christ, perfectly to fulfill the law in the present life' is neither a Pelagian, nor inflicts any injury on the grace of God, nor establishes justification through works." [51] In the end, Arminius does concede that the regenerate person, though he is able, does not actually "'perfectly will' and do that which is good."[52]

Therefore, though the redeemed man is more inclined to do good than in his previous fallen state, he still also has the freedom and the ability to actually do evil. Because men still inhabit their mortal bodies, "They can neither perform any good thing without great resistance and violent struggles, nor abstain from the commission of evil. Nay, it also happens that . . . they sin."[53] Arminius simultaneously teaches that it is possible for man to do good perfectly (*posse non peccare*) and that "even in those who are the most perfect . . . 'in many things . . . offend.'"[54] Though it is possible for redeemed man not to sin, he actually always does commit sin.

Since redeemed man always sins, does he ever sin to the point of completely losing his salvation? The question here concerns the perseverance of the saints—the belief of some that those who have been justified in Christ will never lose their salvation and will necessarily be glorified in heaven at the end of time. In keeping with the free choice doctrine that he holds consistently, Arminius believes that it is possible for redeemed individuals to lose their salvation and not persevere in the grace subsequently applied. These redeemed individuals also possess the free choice to continue in their redeemed condition. Of these redeemed individuals, Arminius declares,

> My sentiments . . . are that those persons who have been grafted into Christ by true faith, and have thus been made partakers of his life-giving Spirit, possess sufficient powers [or strength] to fight against Satan, sin, the world and their own flesh, and to gain the

---

49. Arminius, "Declaration," 1:676–77; see Arminius, "Apology," 2:55.
50. Arminius, "Certain Articles," 2:724 (emphasis added).
51. Ibid., 2:724–25.
52. Arminius, "Romans," 2:541.
53. Arminius, "Public," 2:195.
54. Ibid.

The Views of Free Choice in the Redeemed State

victory over these enemies,—yet not without the assistance of the grace of the same Holy Spirit.[55]

Concerning those who potentially may not persevere, after making a distinction between power (ability) and action (actuality), Arminius says, "And at one time I certainly did say . . . 'that it was possible for believers finally to decline or fall away from faith and salvation.'" He then adds, "But at no period have I asserted 'that believers do finally decline or fall away from faith or salvation.'"[56] Thus, what is possible for believers to do is not to be taken as a affirmation that they actually do or will reject the faith. It is clear from these statements that redeemed man still has the ability and right to rescind salvation accomplished and applied. He still could exercise his free choice and demit salvation. If there is a doctrine of perseverance of the saints here, it is perseverance by default, due to non rescission of salvation, which does not include the thought of being preserved in faith by the special and effectual grace of God. Nevertheless, when his distinction between man's power and action is taken into consideration, it should also be clear that his doctrine of perseverance does not align with the commonly held opinion among calvinists that Arminius believes redeemed persons may in fact lose their salvation. Since the will may never (and has never being known to) exercise its power to rescind salvation, on this matter, Arminius takes a neutral stand.

Again, since Arminius places such an emphasis on the will, we would expect that he would espouse voluntarism. However, he is content to remain an intellectualist. We need not labor long at this point. The trajectory has already been set and by now has become quite predictable. In virtually all the references to intellect/understanding and will we have seen, he places the understanding first. For example, when talking about man in his state of innocence, he points out that it is the understanding that first grasps the clearest vision of God. When talking about man's fall and fallen condition, he teaches that it was the understanding that was principally affected and that it is the understanding that is first liberated by grace. Specifically, when addressing the conversion process, he says that man by "*his Understanding* approves of righteousness."[57]

This gives credence to Muller's assessment that Arminius clearly holds that faith, generally, is the assent given to truth. After distinguishing between that external (beyond the mind) and the internal (in the mind)

---

55. Arminius, "Declaration," 1:664.
56. Arminius, "Apology," 1:741.
57. Arminius, "Public," 2:237; cf. 236.

foundation of faith, Arminius states, "The internal foundation of faith is two-fold,—both the general idea by which we know that God is true,—and the knowledge by which we know that it is the word of God." In the end, he says, "Evangelical faith is an assent of the mind, produced by the Holy Spirit, through the Gospel, in sinners." This assent of the mind is "infused above the order of nature."[58]

When talking about man as redeemed by God, he says of the redeemed man, "He understands the true and saving Good."[59] As Arminius discusses sanctification, he places the emphasis on the mind again when he writes, "First, the mind, which is illuminated, the dark clouds of ignorance being driven away: Next, the inclination or the will [*voluntas*], by which it is delivered from dominion of indwelling sin, and is filled with the Spirit of holiness."[60] In the end, he writes, "The mind, adverse to the flesh, persuades the will [*voluntati*] of man to do that which is holy, and just, and good, and to reject what is merely delectable. . . . The effect produced by the mind on the will [*voluntatem*], is the volition of good and the hatred of evil."[61] Nevertheless, should man demit salvation in this redeemed state, he would be doing so under the guise, mentally, of doing what is good for him—*sub specie bonitatis*.

Conclusion Concerning Redeemed State

The differences between Arminius and Calvin that we encountered in the postlapsarian state persist in the redeemed state, with some slight modifications on some points and mild areas of agreement on other points.

On a note of harmony, Calvin would concur with Arminius that there is a relation between creation and redemption. Calvin would also agree that redemption restores much of what was lost in creation. However—and herein lies a note of disharmony—for Calvin, the re-creation of man in the *imago Dei* in Christ supersedes his originally created condition when it comes to the application of grace.

Contrary to Arminius, when Calvin talks about the re-creation of the *imago Dei* in Christ, he primarily has in view the *imago Dei* in the narrow (spiritual) sense. Thus, the restoration of the image involves the return of true knowledge of God, righteousness, and holiness. It is with the

58. Arminius, "Private," 2:400; cf. Arminius, "Certain Articles," 2:723.
59. Arminius, "Public," 2:194.
60. Arminius, "Private," 2:409; idem, *Opera Theologica*, 318.
61. Arminius, "Romans," 2:583 (emphasis added); idem, *Theologica*, 878.

The Views of Free Choice in the Redeemed State

restoration of the supernatural gifts that man becomes endowed with free choice in the redeemed state. The free choice man possesses is only due to the supernatural work of God. Contrary to Arminius, for Calvin, free choice does not result from anything natural that continues from a previous state into the redeemed state.

In regeneration, for Calvin, God gives man a new disposition of will, not a new will. It is in this new disposition that free choice is located. Witt is therefore wrong when he says, "Calvin's understanding of regeneration conflicts with the Thomist dictum that grace perfects nature rather than supplanting it," as he asserts that Calvin teaches that in regeneration God gives a new will.[62] Witt fails to understand properly what Calvin means when he speaks of the redeemed having a new will.

The free choice that man now possesses enables him to desire and do true spiritual good. This enablement is the primary element of freedom that man receives in the redeemed state. Nevertheless, his voluntary freedom from compulsion remains. Brümmer is incorrect then when he claims that for Calvin grace destroys our freedom from compulsion.[63] Thus, on one level, we may say that Calvin and Arminius believe in the existence of free choice in the redeemed state. However, the power that each ascribes to free choice in the redeemed state is qualitatively different.

Unlike what we have seen with Arminius's nuanced view, Calvin taught the perseverance of the saints. He did not believe redeemed man can lose his salvation. Though he still sins, man can never cast off his garment of salvation given to him in Christ. Though he may fall temporarily, he does not have the free choice to completely forsake his salvation. Thus, for Calvin, true freedom involves more than the freedom of contrary choice or indifference. True freedom of choice is the free choice to pursue and do spiritual good. Man's will in the redeemed state is now irrevocably bound in the direction of goodness.

Naturally, then, Calvin continues to maintain a voluntarist view in the redeemed state, contrary to Arminius's intellectualism. This is seen in Calvin's emphasis upon the will in redemption and sanctification. I therefore disagree with Kendall and agree with Muller, who concludes that Calvin's voluntarist leaning is not pure voluntarism but a "soteriological voluntarism."[64]

---

62. Witt, "Creation," 97.
63. Brümmer, "Calvin, Bernard," 452.
64. Muller, "*Fides* and *Cognitio*," 223.

How does Arminius's view of man's will in the redeemed state compare with Calvin's view? Arminius also sees a connection between creation and redemption. Thus, redemption is, in a large measure, a restoration of what was lost in the fall. However, in Arminius's teaching, the *imago Dei* that is restored in redemption relates to both the natural (intellect, will, and affections) and supernatural (knowledge, righteousness, and holiness) aspects of man. As we have seen in a previous chapter, free choice is bound up with the natural gifts. Therefore, man does not receive free choice anew in redemption. Free choice only becomes freer than it was. It is enabled more to do the good because of the believers' continued cooperation with grace. It is in this sense that free choice is saved.

Therefore, Bangs's assessment of Arminius, that redeemed man possesses a free will (choice) apart from nature, is incorrect. Though there is the far superior supernatural gift of grace through Christ, which grants man freedom of choice, by virtue of Arminius's doctrine of creation of man, which still holds true, there continues to be a significant sense in which redeemed man has free choice by virtue of his natural endowment, which is maintained through providence. This free choice is made better in redemption.

The grace of redemption, however, is no different in quality from the pre-fall, providential, and prevenient grace. This redemptive grace provides no guarantee that the believer will persevere and be preserved in salvation. Though man is more inclined to do spiritual good, he still has the power of free choice to reject and cast off his garment of salvation. Whether any person has or will lose his or her salvation is left unanswered. The most Arminius confirms on this point is that he never does say true believers actually lose their salvation; they are only able.

Should a believer refuse to persevere in salvation, this would still be done from an intellectualist standpoint. Since it is part of the nature of man always to be inclined to do good, the will would still be acting in obedience to the deceived intellect. However, should a believer choose to persist and persevere in his salvation, this would occur as the mind continues to give its assent in faith. As Muller has shown, Arminius identifies faith primarily as knowledge and assent while relegating trust—the part of faith that involves the will—to be the consequence of faith as opposed to part of the substance of faith.[65]

---

65. Muller, "Priority," 61.

Chapter 4

The Views of Free Choice in the Glorified State

Calvin: Man's Choice Is Completely Free

THERE IS VERY LITTLE in the secondary and primary literature on this area of our study. Perhaps this is only natural, considering that the glorified state is the most distant to our present experience. Moreover, those who have experienced that state of affairs in glory, however limited, have not returned to inform us about the nature and function of the will in glory. Nevertheless, we do have some clear statements from Calvin that assist us in understanding how he thought about the will and its function in the glorified state.

An important matter to consider at the outset concerns the issue of the chief good of man. Calvin says, "Concerning the chief good: none however, except Plato, acknowledged that it consisted in union with God."[1] Since heaven is the place where all of God's elect saints experience their chief good, it follows that in heaven man will experience an increased measure of union with God over that which he now experiences through Christ.

Calvin further supports this view of what heaven consists of by quoting from Psalm 17:15, which reads, "I shall be satisfied when I awake in your likeness," and 2 Peter 1:4, which describes the purpose of the believer's life to be that of "partaking in the Divine nature." Calvin goes on to say, "If our Lord will share his glory, power, and righteousness with the elect, nay will give himself to be enjoyed by them; and what is better still, will, in a manner, become one with them, let us remember that every kind of

---

1. Calvin, *Institutes*, III.xxv.2.

happiness is herein included."[2] Calvin does have a sense that man was created for the end of union with God—a union that will be fully consummated in the final state of the believer's eternal existence.

In this final expression of the union with God and man which properly began in Christ, the qualities that were lost in the fall are perfectly renewed and regained in glory. It is quite natural, then, for us to reflect on areas of continuity in Calvin's thought between man's situation in the first paradise of Eden and man's situation in the last paradise of heaven. Calvin highlights the continuity between man as he was originally created and the situation of man in glory when, after stating that the image of God was "almost destroyed" in the fall and is now "partly seen in the elect," he says, "its full luster, however, will be displayed in heaven."[3] The *imago Dei* brightly existed in Adam in his pre-fall state. The *imago Dei* was so ruined in the fall that it was almost destroyed. In Christ, brighter glimmerings of the *imago Dei* began to show themselves again in the elect. Therefore, with good inference, we may conclude that the full luster of the *imago Dei* that is gained in heaven includes, at least, the complete restoration and supreme perfection of the body and the faculties of the soul, which include intellect, will, and affections, and the most perfect restoration and supreme function of the supernatural gifts of knowledge, righteousness, and holiness.

Thus, the freedom of choice that man will possess in the glorified state is a freedom only to do good—*non posse peccare*—considering that there will be no possibility of temptation by evil. Here too the understanding, which began to function appropriately in redemption by presenting known good to the will, realizes and perfects its role—in keeping with the dictum that *grace restores nature*.[4] Therefore, the understanding, being perfected, will only and forever always present absolute good to the will to choose. The will, having itself been perfected, will always and forever choose the perfect good which the intellect presents.

One of the claims Pighius made against Calvin is that he transfers a future condition of the saints to the present situation of the saints when he teaches that man in the redeemed state is able not to sin. In his response, Calvin defends bringing "the future condition after the resurrection" of the saints at the end of time to bear upon the state of redeemed believer in this life. "For," as Calvin continues, "now there begins in the saints what

2. Ibid., III.xxv.10.
3. Ibid., I.xv.4.
4. Calvin, *Bondage*, 99, 155, 212.

will then be fully completed."[5] For Calvin, regeneration restores only part of man's freedom. The complete and full restoration of man's freedom takes place in glory. All that was said concerning the positive blessings of redemption may then be applied to and be magnified in the glorified state. Therefore, since one of the blessings of redemption had to do with our release from total bondage to sin—an act that restored free choice in part—we may logically infer that complete and full freedom of choice is present only when there is freedom from the possibility of sinning.[6] Thus, for Calvin, paradise lost is not merely regained in the heavenly state; it is made far better—the best in can ever be. This is perfection.

Since this is the case for Calvin—that the will and the intellect will arrive at perfection—it follows that their proper function in relation to each other will also be perfectly restored. Hence, in light of my position that Calvin moved to a voluntarist viewpoint primarily because of the introduction of sin in the world and retained a voluntarist concept while sin was still present, now that sin has been eradicated, the intellectualist position reasserts its priority as man's will for eternity obeys the beck and call of reason. The voluntaristic crack that, according to Hoitenga, Calvin opened in order to explain the fall completely closes at this point.

Therefore, I believe that Calvin is consistent when all four states (pure nature, fallen nature, redeemed nature, and glorified nature) are taken into consideration. Muller's suggested "symmetrical model" (intellectualism in the first and the last state and voluntarism in the two middle ones) supports this consistency.[7]

Arminius: Man's Choice Is Completely Free

We have now come to the point of looking at Arminius's view of man's freedom of choice in the glorified state. And as we have seen with Calvin, in considering this state, there is a dearth of information both in the primary and secondary literature with respect also to Arminius. As we embark upon addressing Arminius's view of the will in the glorified state, quite naturally some elements that have been part of our discussion thus far will fade into the background and disappear.

---

5. Ibid., 241–42; see Lane, *Student*, 185.
6. Calvin, *Bondage*, 242.
7. Muller, "Foreword," 6.

As I seek to ascertain from the little information available from the writings of Arminius on the state of the will in glory, a summary review of Arminius's view of God's relation to humankind is in order. When I broached the subject of Arminius's view of the will in the prelapsarian situation, I took the time to discuss how his view of God and his relation to the creature affected Arminius's view of the nature of the human will and free choice. We have seen that, for Arminius, the goal of theology is the eternal blessedness of man in union with God.[8]

All throughout our discussion, we have seen that God's relation to the rational creature is integral to Arminius's understanding of the human will and free choice. Since God possesses the faculties of intellect and will and has perfect free choice, by virtue of creating man in his own image, God unites himself with man (the goal of theology practically considered) in such a way that he communicates the faculties of understanding and will to the creature and blesses him with the ability to make genuinely free human choices.

However, since our union with God which began in creation is still incomplete in Christ, it follows that the place of the completion of this union is in heaven with God. In heaven, glorified man sees God as he is. Arminius says as much when he states, "For in union with Him [God] consists the bliss of rational creatures."[9] And to Gomarus he says, "Salvation or eternal life is union with God."[10]

It seems, then, that in the glorified state, where sin and its effects are absent, the qualities man lost in the fall and started to regain in Christ in the redeemed state now logically become his. This goal of theology—union with God—is achieved in the glorified state according to man's created capability. Here, man finally becomes what he was created to become.

Thus far, my argument has been mainly logical. Nevertheless, this view can be substantiated from Arminius's actual writings. In one of his disputations, after giving five senses in which freedom may be understood, Arminius, speaking of the freedom from misery, says, "The freedom [*libertas*] from misery, which agreed with man when recently created and not fallen into sin, will again be in accordance with him when he shall be translated in body and soul into celestial blessedness."[11] In the glorified state, man in

---

8. Muller, *God, Creation*, 77.
9. Arminius, "Perkins's," 3:277.
10. Arminius, "Gomarus," 3:591.
11. Arminius, "Public," 2:190; idem, *Opera Theologica*, 210.

The Views of Free Choice in the Glorified State

all his faculties will be free from misery, which is the natural consequence of being free from sin and all its effects.

Arminius continues, "But about these two modes also, of freedom [*libertate*] from necessity and from misery, we have here no dispute." Concerning freedom from necessity—another way of speaking of free choice in his understanding—Arminius argues that this always agrees with man "because it is by nature situated in the will [*voluntati*], as its proper attribute, so that there cannot be any will [*voluntas*] if it is not free [*libera*]."[12] Again he says, "By his [God's], free-will [*liberam voluntatem*], all his volitions and actions concerning the creatures agree with his nature, and that immutably; because he willed [*voluit*] at the same time, that they [God's volitions and actions] should not be retracted or repealed."[13] Keep in mind that Arminius locates free choice in the faculty of the will.

Therefore, the point is that, inasmuch as freedom from necessity was not revoked in the fall *because of the immutability* of God and because of the created relation that exists between him and his creatures, it is only natural then to conclude that this freedom of choice obtains even more in the glorified state, where nature as created is perfected. For Arminius, freedom of will necessarily and always entails freedom of choice.

Glorification is the end of the process, begun in creation, where man actualizes his created potential. It is safe to conclude that the glorified will is free from sin and its dominion. This is the case in light of what glory is—a place where sin will be no more.

In this state of perfection, the intellect will fully reign over a will that is perfectly able, willing, and ready to submit to the good direction of the intellect. Therefore, Arminius necessarily holds to a priority of the intellect over the will in the glorified state. This is only natural in light of his theology. A quotation of his worth repeating at this point occurs when he teaches that the "rational creature . . . cannot rest except in the greatest union of itself with God." He then adds, implying that the rest takes place in glory where the union with God will be complete, that "By this union, the understanding beholds in the clearest vision . . . God himself, and all his goodness and incomparable beauty."[14] Thus, Muller is correct when he states, "Arminius appears to stress the intellectual vision of God as the primary characteristic of blessedness and to understand the affective cleaving to God as a cor-

---

12. Arminius, "Public," 2:190; idem, *Opera Theologica*, 210.
13. Arminius, "Oration III," 1:377–78; idem, *Opera Theologica*, 48.
14. Arminius, "Oration II," 1:362–63.

respondent characteristic, dependent in some sense upon the intellectual vision." Muller further points out that Arminius's intellectualism "perfectly reproduces the classic intellectualist thesis of Thomas Aquinas."[15] It is safe, then, to apply Fredrick Copleston's words about Aquinas's intellectualism to Arminius. For Arminius, "when the soul sees the essence of God immediately, the intrinsic superiority of intellect to will reasserts itself."[16]

Conclusion Concerning Glorified State

Perhaps there is rapprochement after all! What was impossible on earth is now a reality in glory. It appears that, from the little that could be gathered, Calvin and Arminius are in significant agreement with respect to the nature and function of the will in the glorified state. However, it seems they would still differ on the reasons for the existence of free choice and on how it exists in or with the soul.

Like Arminius, Calvin affirms that the chief good for man consists in eternal blessedness and union (full communion) with God. But for Calvin, this union began primarily in Christ. Thus, the experience of glory will fully satisfy the taste of blessedness we now have in Christ.

Calvin also maintains, in agreement with Arminius, that the *imago Dei* lost in the fall is restored to perfection in the glorified state. The luster of the image includes the complete restoration of the faculties of intellect and will and their proper function. In glory, man still has a will (*voluntas*) that is free; he is still free from compulsion. In addition, he now possesses an unfettered free choice (*arbitrium*) to do only spiritual good, which constitutes worshipping God and enjoying him forever. Contrary to Arminius, the free choice man experiences in glory is not at all merely theoretical (see below), considering that for Calvin true freedom of choice entails being free to do only good. Like Arminius, for Calvin ultimate free choice entails the impossibility of sinning—*non posse peccare*.

Finally, in glory, since what was lost in creation is regained and restored, we have seen that the proper function of the priority of the intellect over the will, again, becomes the norm. Moreover, since Calvin shifts to voluntarism because of the introduction of sin, it is natural to expect that, with the absence of sin, he would logically return to his original prelapsarian stance of intellectualism.

15. Muller, *God, Creation*, 77, 78.
16. Copleston, *History of Philosophy*, 383.

The Views of Free Choice in the Glorified State

Arminius affirms that the goal of creational theology, which is union with God, finally achieves its consummation in the glorified state. Here in heaven, redeemed people, who were faithful in continuing to cooperate with grace, experience eternal bliss. The redeemed inclination toward the good finally receives its reward.

Part of the bliss the redeemed experience in glory is freedom from sin and its effects. Because of the immutability of God, the redeemed still possess freedom of will (*voluntas*) which, in Arminius's understanding, necessarily entails free choice (*arbitrium*). In light of Arminius's view of creation and its impact on man's will, and since free choice always requires real choice between good and evil, to maintain this kind of free choice in glory would require a measure of inconsistency on the part of Arminius. For if there is no sin nor the possibility of sinning in glory, how can there be genuine choice? Therefore, his view of the irrevocability of man's free choice places him in a conundrum at this point. Perhaps free choice as he explains it becomes a theoretical construct. If there were evil, man would be able to choose it. The free choice—as Arminius understands it—that man has in glory is not actual but is a theoretical fiction.

Be that as it may, he is still able consistently to maintain an intellectualist view of man in the glorified state without doing injustice to his particular system of theology on the nature of the will.

Conclusion

ON THE BASIS OF this comparative study of Calvin's and Arminius's views of the human will in the fourfold state of man, we have seen that they are in general agreement concerning the function of man's free choice in the prelapsarian and glorified states and are in particular disagreement about the function of man's free choice in the postlapsarian and redeemed states of man. With respect to the nature and location of man's free choice, there is a persistent disagreement between Calvin and Arminius in all four states of man.

In our look at the prelapsarian state, we have seen that for Calvin and Arminius there are some points of agreement with respect to the existence and function of free choice. However, they differ on the reason for and the mode of existence of free choice in the state of innocence. On another point of difference between Calvin and Arminius, we have seen that creation does not play as pivotal a role for Calvin as it does in the theology of Arminius on the matter of free choice. Calvin's purpose for teaching about creation is not primarily to address union with God as the goal of creation. Rather than speaking about man's creation in the image of God as a mode of union, Calvin sees man as a true representation (*imago*) of God (*Dei*). Contrary to Arminius, this representation is seen primarily in the exercise of the supernatural gifts rather than in the natural gifts, though the natural gifts reflect the image of God in a broader sense.

By refraining from discussing union with God apart from Christ and by making the image of God relate to the supernatural gifts, Calvin closes the door—left open in Arminius's view of the created will—to natural theology. For Calvin, the creation of man in the image of God is much more about equipping man with the gifts necessary for him to fulfill his office as covenant head than it is about union in the Arminian sense.

In Calvin, original free choice is sufficient to render human beings inexcusable before God when they are justly condemned. Calvin agrees with Arminius that man's misuse of his free choice is the cause of the fall. Calvin goes a step further and argues that the fall was a necessary result of the Divine decree. Arminius is unwilling to go that far.

In the original state, for Calvin, man had the ability to choose freely between doing good and evil. Though he agrees with Arminius on this point, he differs from Arminius in the location of man's free choice. For Arminius, free choice exists with the natural gifts, whereas for Calvin it exists with the supernatural gifts. For Calvin, the natural gifts are gifts of God's general grace in creation and the supernatural gifts pertain to his particular grace in redemption.

With respect to Arminius, his understanding of God, creation, and the relation between them significantly shapes his view of the nature of human choice in all four states of man. In the prelapsarian state, where union with God is the goal, God creates man in his image with freedom of choice—as much free choice as is suited to his created capacity. Freedom of choice is located in the natural part of man and, as such, is an essential part of the nature of man. Man's misuse of his freedom of choice is the cause of the fall. Arminius attributes the cause of the fall to man's free choice in order to vindicate God's justice and free him from the charge of being the author of sin.

Similar to Calvin's view, being endowed with free choice, man is able to choose to do spiritual good or evil. However, in the state of original perfection, he is more at liberty to do good than to do evil. Although man is able to make genuine free choices, such choices are made out of deference to the intellect's good judgment. Thus, for Arminius, in the prelapsarian state, the intellect has priority.

When we looked at Calvin's and Arminius's views of man's will in the postlapsarian state, we saw many more points of difference between them. Both theologians acknowledge that the natural aspects of man's creation persist in a corrupted form in the fallen state and that the supernatural gifts have been taken away. They differ on the nature of the severity of the corruption of the natural gifts. For Calvin, the corruption of nature is much more radical than it is in Arminius's understanding. Since both men aver strongly in favor of man's corruption and depravity, this difference in severity must be attributed to where each theologian locates free choice and not simply to the effects of sin, since both argue that the effects of sin upon fallen man were severe. The real point of difference is that, for Arminius, the natural gifts, which were not destroyed but persist after the fall, include free choice. Man therefore has free choice in the fallen state in light of nature and in light of prevenient, providential, and redemptive grace in Christ.

Calvin, though he concedes that the natural gifts endure in a severely corrupted state in the fall, locates free choice in the supernatural gifts. Hence, since the supernatural gifts have been taken away in the fall, fallen man does not possess freedom of choice. Man is bound by the fetters of sin. He commits sin voluntarily, but necessarily and without compulsion.

Since free choice does not endure, for Calvin, man can do no spiritual good, nor does he desire true spiritual good. Hence, he cannot cooperate in the salvation process, and without the effectual working of God's special grace—given only to the elect—he cannot respond positively to the gospel. On the other hand, Arminius sees no qualitative difference between prelapsarian grace and postlapsarian grace. Since sin has been introduced into the world, Calvin assumes a voluntarist stance in the fallen state. Here, the will acts according to the desire of the flesh.

However, since free choice continues in the fallen state, according to Arminius, man is able to do true spiritual good that is pleasing to God. Free choice, again, protects God from the charge of being the author of sin and vindicates his justice and goodness in man's condemnation. With the right exercise of free choice, all people are able to cooperate with God in the process of salvation. Men have the power to reject or accept the internal call of special grace. We may think of Arminius's view of grace in two ways. First, Arminius's grace is never effectual to bring about salvation. Second, grace for Arminius is always effectual, properly understood, since the purpose of grace is not to cause salvation but only to make the choosing of salvation possible. Its effectiveness falls short of persuading a positive response to the gospel. Should man accept the call of the gospel, he does so primarily through an act of the intellect, which has priority in the fallen state.

In our consideration of the redeemed state, we have seen that Calvin agrees with Arminius that redeemed man possesses free choice to desire and perform spiritual good and evil. However, Calvin vehemently denies that man is able to exercise his free choice in such a way as to relinquish his salvation.

With respect to Arminius, we saw that he believes man continues to have free choice to choose between good and evil by virtue of creation and by virtue of redemptive grace. As a result, man becomes freer. Through Christ, much of what is lost is restored. However, the free choice that man still possesses enables him to relinquish his salvation. It is ultimately up to man to determine, by the use of free choice enlightened by grace, whether he will remain in salvation accomplished and applied. Whether man chooses to give up or to remain in salvation, he acts in subjection to the intellect, which continues to have priority over the will.

In the analysis of the glorified state, we have seen that Calvin and Arminius are virtually agreed in many matters relating to the will. They both affirm that union with God, according to their respective understanding of union, constitutes the ultimate blessing for redeemed man. They agree that, in heaven, man will become all that he was created and meant to be.

In the glorified state, free choice exists. For Calvin, the ultimate expression of free choice is the freedom to do only good—a freedom that human beings possess in the glorified state. In this way, human beings, to the extent that they—as creatures—are able, perfectly represent God, who also possesses freedom to do only the good. Since sin and evil will be absent, I am not sure how Arminius would characterize this free choice, considering that, for him, free choice involves the ability to choose between good and evil.

In this book, I have tried to clarify exactly what is meant when the term "free will" is used. At least, I have shown that the heart of the discussion concerning free will is really about the freedom of choice to do spiritual good that is pleasing to God and has salvific merit. It appears that part of the reason why there are divergent views within some of the scholarly literature dealing with each theologian's views is due to a lack of precision when it comes to the use of the term "free will," which, depending on the context, may refer to free choice (the function) or to free will (the faculty).

In addition, I have shown that any discussion of the matter of free choice, particularly as it relates to Calvin, must be sensitive to the various states of man. Simply to say that one theologian believes man possesses or does not possess free choice, without reference to a particular state of man's existence, is often not helpful. Lane is absolutely correct when he concludes that, if the different stages of man's history are not taken into consideration, not even Calvin could give a clear answer to the question, "Did Calvin believe in free will?"[1] Though Arminius could give a very clear affirmative answer (considering that he maintained that man possessed free will in all four states of man) were Lane's question addressed to him, it is still very helpful to look

---

1. Lane, "Did Calvin?," 86.

at his affirmative answer in light of the fourfold state in order to appreciate the various nuances that he applies to free choice in each state of man.

Another contribution of this book to the discussion of free will (choice) is that it highlights more clearly how pivotal the location of free choice within man is to any discussion of free choice as it relates to Calvin and Arminius. Thus, the heart of the issue does not revolve around whether Arminius or Calvin believed, in concept, *that* man has free will. Man is a free agent who acts freely and without compulsion. As we have shown, when all the states of man are taken into consideration, Arminius believes man possesses free choice in all the states of man. Calvin, on the other hand believes that man possesses varying degrees of free choice in three of the states of man. Only in the fallen state does Calvin advocate the bondage of the will (choice) to sin. And even here, in the fallen state, Calvin cautiously allows for the use of the term "free choice" in a very restricted and minimalist sense, where all that is meant by free choice is that man acts voluntarily without compulsion or coercion. Therefore, when all the states of man are taken into consideration, it may be said that Calvin believes more in the freedom of the will (choice) than in its bondage. But looking at the matter in this way would make it appear that there is very little difference between Arminius and Calvin on the matter of free will and choice.

However, if we move beyond simply asking whether or not man has free will/choice and focus the debate, with due consideration to each state of man, on *how* man came to possess free choice in light of God's decrees, creation, providence, and redemption, on *where* exactly free choice is to be located in relation to man's soul, on *why* free choice exists or does not exists in particular states of man, and on *what* powers ought to be ascribed to free choice, it becomes very evident that Arminius and Calvin differ significantly. They not only differ significantly; they differ on the significant issues relating to the function of God's grace in the conversion of man and to the extent of man's cooperation or lack thereof in the process of salvation. Only when we proceed with sensitivity to the questions posed above are we able to give clearer answers to a long-standing and much-debated issue.

Finally, then, in my view, if indeed the advocates of both systems desire to preserve the essence of Calvinism or Arminianism, the fundamental differences between the systems of theology advocated by Arminius and Calvin are such that all attempts to reconcile the two theological systems in this life will prove to be a work in futility. Indeed, Arminius's theological system is an alternative to that of Calvin—at least with respect to the nature

Conclusion

of the human will in the fourfold state of man.[2] On the subject of the nature of the will, we find Arminius's thought to be more in continuity with the Thomistic tradition than with the Reformed tradition.

---

2. Muller, "Gambit," 262; see also ibid., 254, 227; Muller, "Christological," 146; and Muller, "Federal Motif," 102–3.

Bibliography

Alexander, Archibald. *Theories of the Will in the History of Philosophy.* New York: Scribner's, 1898.
Ames, William. *The Marrow of Theology.* Translated by John Dykstra Eusden. Grand Rapids: Baker, 1997.
Aquinas, Thomas. *Basic Writings of Saint Thomas Aquinas.* Edited by Anton C. Pegis. 1 vol. New York: Random House, 1945.
Arendt, Hannah. *The Life of the Mind: Willing.* New York: Harcourt Brace Jovanovich, 1978.
Arminius, James (Jacobus). "The Apology or Defense of James Arminius." In *The Works of James Arminius,* 1:733–70 and 2:1–63.
———. "Certain Articles to Be Diligently Examined and Weighed." In *The Works of James Arminius,* 2:706–31.
———. "A Declaration of the Sentiments of Arminius." In *The Works of James Arminius,* 1:580–732.
———. "A Dissertation on the True and Genuine Sense of the Seventh Chapter of St. Paul's Epistle to the Romans." In *The Works of James Arminius,* 2:471–688.
———. "Examination of the Theses of Dr. Francis Gomarus Respecting Predestination." In *The Works of James Arminius,* 3:521–658.
———. "Friendly Conference with Dr. Francis Junius." In *The Works of James Arminius,* 3:1–248.
———. "A Letter to Hippolytus a Collibus." In *The Works of James Arminius,* 2:689–705.
———. "Modest Examination of Dr. Perkins's Pamphlet." In *The Works of James Arminius,* 3:249–484.
———. *Opera Theologica.* Leiden: Godefridum Basson, 1629.
———. *Opera Theologica.* 2nd ed. Frankfurt: Wolfgangum Hoffmannum, 1635.
———. "Oration I." In *The Works of James Arminius,* 1:321–47.
———. "Oration II." In *The Works of James Arminius,* 1:348–73.
———. "Oration III." In *The Works of James Arminius,* 1:374–401.
———. "The Private Disputations of James Arminius on the Principal Articles of the Christian Religion." In *The Works of James Arminius,* 2:318–469.

Bibliography

———. "The Public Disputations of James Arminius." In *The Works of James Arminius*, 2:72–317.

———. *The Works of James Arminius*. Translated by James Nichols and William Nichols. 3 vols. Grand Rapids: Baker, 1996. Originally published: London: Longman et al., 1825, 1828, 1875.

Armstrong, Brian G. "*Duplex Cognitio Dei*, Or? The Problem and Relation of Structure, Form, and Purpose in Calvin's Theology." In *Probing the Reformed Tradition: Historical Studies in Honor of Edward A. Dowey, Jr.*, eds. Elsie Anne McKee and Brian G. Armstrong, 135–153. Louisville: John Knox, 1989.

Asselt, Willem J. van, J. Martin Bac, and Roelf T. te Velde, editors. *Reformed Thought on Freedom: The Concept of Free Choice in Early Modern Reformed Theology*. Grand Rapids: Baker Academic, 2010.

Augustine, Arelius. *Saint Augustine: Eighty-Three Different Questions*. Translated by David L. Mosher. Washington, DC: Catholic University of America Press, 1982.

———. *Saint Augustine: Four Anti-Pelagian Writings*. Translated by John A. Mourant and William J. Collinge. Washington, DC: Catholic University of America Press, 1992.

———. *Saint Augustine: The Retractions*. Translated by Mary Inez Bogan. Washington, DC: Catholic University of America Press, 1968.

———. *Saint Augustine: The Teacher; The Free Choice of The Will*. Translated by Robert P. Russell. Washington, DC: Catholic University of America Press, 1968.

Bangs, Carl. *Arminius: A Study in the Dutch Reformation*. Grand Rapids: Zondervan, 1985.

———. "Arminius and Reformed Theology." PhD diss., University of Chicago, 1958.

———. "Arminius and the Reformation." *Church History* 30 (1961) 155–70.

———. "Arminius as a Reformed Theologian." In *The Heritage of John Calvin*, edited by John H. Bratt, 209–22. Grand Rapids: Eerdmans, 1973.

———. *The Auction Catalogue of the Library of J. Arminius*. Utrecht: Hes, 1985.

———. "Introduction." In *The Works of James Arminius*, 1:vii–xxix.

Bergvall, Åke. "Reason in Luther, Calvin, and Sidney." *SixteenthCentury Journal* 23/1 (1992) 115–27.

Berkhof, Louis. *Systematic Theology*. Reprint, Grand Rapids: Eerdmans, 1979.

Blacketer, Raymond A. "Arminius' Concept of Covenant in Its Historical Context." *Nederlands Archief voor Kerkgeschiedenis* 80/2 (2000) 193–220.

Bonansea, Bernardine M. "Duns Scotus Voluntarism." In *John Duns Scotus, 1265–1965*, edited by John K. Ryan and Bernardine M. Bonansea, 83–121. Washington, DC: Catholic University of America Press, 1965.

Boston, Thomas. *Human Nature in Its Fourfold State*. 1720. Reprint, London: Banner of Truth Trust, 1964.

Bourke, Vernon. *Will in Western Thought: A Historical-Critical Survey*. New York: Sheed & Ward, 1964.

Boyd, Gregory A. *God of the Possible: A Biblical Introduction to the Open View of God*. Grand Rapids: Baker, 2000.

Brandt, Casper. *The Life of James Arminius*. Translated by John Guthrie. Nashville: E. Stevenson & F. A. Owen, 1857.

Brown, William Kenneth. "An Analysis of Romans 7 with an Evaluation of Arminius' Dissertation on Romans 7." PhD diss., Bob Jones University, 1984.

Brümmer, Vincent. "Calvin, Bernard and the Freedom of the Will." *Religious Studies* 30 (1994) 437–55.

BIBLIOGRAPHY

Bryant, Barry E. "Molina, Arminius, Plaifere, Goad, and Wesley on Human Free-Will, Divine Omniscience, and Middle Knowledge." *Wesleyan Theological Journal* 27 (spring–fall 1992) 93–103.

Calvin, John. *The Bondage and Liberation of the Will: A Defense of the Orthodox Doctrine of Human Choice against Pighius.* Translated by G. I. Davies, edited by Anthony S. Lane. Grand Rapids: Baker, 1996.

———. *Concerning the Eternal Predestination of God.* Translated by J. K. S. Reid. London: James Clarke, 1961.

———. *Ezekiel. Calvin's Commentaries*, vols. 11, 12. Translated by Thomas Meyers. Grand Rapids: Baker, 1979.

———. *Genesis. Calvin's Commentaries*, vol. 1. Translated by John King. Grand Rapids: Baker, 1979.

———. *Institutes of the Christian Religion.* Translated by Ford Lewis Battles. 2 vols. Philadelphia: Westminster, 1960.

———. *Institutes of the Christian Religion.* Translated by Henry Beveridge. Grand Rapids: Eerdmans, 1989.

———. *Romans. Calvin's Commentaries*, vol. 19. Translated by John Owen. Grand Rapids: Baker, 1979.

———. *Selected Works of John Calvin: Tracts and Letters.* Translated by Henry Beveridge. 3 vols. Grand Rapids: Baker, 1983.

———. *Sermons on Deuteronomy.* Carlisle, PA: Banner of Truth Trust, 1987.

———. *Treatises Against the Anabaptists and Against the Libertines.* Translated by Benjamin Wirt Farley. Grand Rapids: Baker, 1982.

Calvini, Ioannis. *Opera Quae Supersunt Omnia.* Edited by Guilielmus Baum, Eduardus Cunitz, and Eduardus Ruess. Vols. 2–40. Brunsvigale: C. A. Schwetschke et Filium (M. Bruhn), 1863–89.

Cameron, Charles A. "Arminius—Hero or Heretic?" *Evangelical Quarterly* 64/3 (1992) 213–27.

Chalker, William H. "Calvin and Some Seventeenth-Century Calvinists: A Comparison of Their Thought through an Examination of Their Doctrines of the Knowledge of God, Faith and Assurance." PhD diss., Duke University, 1961.

Clarke, F. Stuart. "Arminius's Understanding of Calvin." *Evangelical Quarterly* 54 (January–March 1982) 25–35.

———. "The Theology of Arminius." *London Quarterly and Holborn Review* 185 (October 1960) 248–53.

Compier, Don H. "The Independent Pupil: Calvin's Transformation of Erasmus' Theological Hermeneutics." *Westminster Theological Journal* 54 (1992) 217–33.

Copleston, Frederick. *A History of Philosophy.* 9 vols. Garden City, NY: Image Books, 1985.

Crabtree, J. A. "Does Middle Knowledge Solve the Problem of Divine Sovereignty?" In *The Grace of God, the Bondage of the Will*, edited by Thomas R. Schreiner and Bruce A. Ware, 2: 429–457. Grand Rapids: Baker, 1995.

Craig, William L. "Middle Knowledge: A Calvinist-Arminian Rapprochement?" In *The Grace of God, the Will of Man: A Case for Arminianism*, edited by Clark H. Pinnock, 141–64. Grand Rapids: Zondervan, 1989.

Cunningham, William. *Historical Theology.* Vol. 1. Great Britain: Banner of Truth Trust, 1969.

Dekker, Eef. "Jacobus Arminius and His Logic: Analysis of a Letter." *Journal of Theological Studies* 44 (April 1993) 118–42.

Bibliography

———. "Was Arminius a Molinist?" *Sixteenth Century Journal* 27/2 (1996) 337–52.

Dell, Robert Thomas. "Man's Freedom and Bondage in the Thought of Martin Luther and James Arminius." PhD diss., Boston University, 1962.

Boer, William den. *God's Twofold Love: The Theology of Jacob Arminius (1559–1609)*. Translated by Albert Gootjes. Germany: Vandenhoeck & Ruprecht, 2010.

———. "Jacobus Arminius: Theologian of God's Twofold Love." In *Arminius, Arminianism, and Europe: Jacobus Arminius (1559/60–1609)*, edited by Theodoor Marius Van Leeuwen, Keith D. Stanglin, and Marijke Tolsma, 25–50. Leiden: Brill, 2009.

Dielhe, Albrecht. *The Theory of Will in Classical Antiquity*. Berkeley: University of California Press. 1982.

Donnelly, John Patrick. "Calvinist Thomism." *Viator: Medieval and Renaissance Studies* 7 (1976) 441–55.

Dorner, I. A. *History of Protestant Theology*. 2 vols. Edinburgh: T. & T. Clark, 1871.

Dow, Thomas Edward. "The Evangelical Ecumenism of James Arminius." PhD diss., University of Waterloo (Canada), 1981.

Dowey, Edward A., Jr. *The Knowledge of God in Calvin's Theology*. Grand Rapids: Eerdmans, 1994.

Du Moulin, Pierre. *The Anatomy of Arminianism: Or the Opening of the Controversies Lately Handled in the Low Countries, Concerning the Doctrine of Predestination, of the Death of Christ, of the Nature of Grace*. London, 1620.

Edwards, Paul, editor. *Encyclopedia of Philosophy*. 8 vols. New York: Macmillian, 1967.

Elwell, Walter A., editor. *The Concise Evangelical Dictionary of Theology*. Grand Rapids: Baker, 1991.

Engel, Mary Potter. *John Calvin's Perspectival Anthropology*. Edited by Susan Thistlethwaite. Atlanta: Scholars', 1988.

Erasmus, Desiderius. *The Essential Erasmus*. Translated by John P. Dolan. New York: Meridian, 1964.

Feinberg, John S. "The Doctrine of Human Freedom in the Writings of John Calvin." Th.M. thesis, Trinity Evangelical Divinity School at Deerfield, 1972.

———. "God, Freedom, and Evil in Calvinist Thinking." In *The Grace of God, the Bondage of the Will*, edited by Thomas R. Schreiner and Bruce A. Ware, 2:459–483. Grand Rapids: Baker, 1995.

Fesko, John V. "Arminius on *Facientibus Quod in se Est* and Likely Medieval Sources." In *Church and School in Early Modern Protestantism: Studies in Honor of Richard A. Muller on the Maturation of a Theological Tradition*, edited by Jordan J. Ballor, David S. Sytsma, and Jason Zuidema, 347–60. Leiden: Brill, 2013.

Forlines, F. Leroy. *Classical Arminianism: A Theology of Salvation*. Nashville: Randall House, 2011.

Gerstner, John H. "Augustine, Luther, Calvin, and Edwards on the Bondage of the Will." In *The Grace of God, the Bondage of the Will*, edited by Thomas R. Schreiner and Bruce A. Ware, 279–95. Grand Rapids: Baker, 1995.

Gilson, Etiene. *The Christian Philosophy of St. Thomas Aquinas*. New York: Random House, 1956.

———. *History of Christian Philosophy in the Middle Ages*. New York: Random House, 1955.

———. *The Philosophy of Saint Thomas Aquinas*. Translated by Edward Bullough. New York: Dorset, 1948.

Bibliography

———. *The Spirit of Medieval Philosophy*. Translated by A. H. C. Downes. New York: Scribner's, 1940.

Girardeau, John L. *The Will in Its Theological Relations*. New York: Baker & Taylor, 1891.

Gunter, W. Stephen. *Arminius and His Declaration of Sentiments: An Annotated Translation with Introduction and Theological Commentary*. Waco, TX: Baylor University, 2012.

Hagenbach, K. R. *A Text Book of the History of Doctrines*. Translated by Henry B. Smith. 2 vols. New York: Sheldon & Co., 1872.

Harper, George W. "Calvin and English Calvinism." *Calvin Theological Journal* 20 (1985) 255–62.

Harrison, A. W. *Arminianism*. London: Kemp Hall, 1937.

Hazen, Harry Booth. "Calvin's Doctrine of Faith." PhD diss., University of Chicago, 1903.

Headley, Alrick G. "The Nature of the Will in the Writings of Calvin and Arminius: A Comparative Study." ThM thesis, Calvin Theological Seminar at Grand Rapids, 2004.

Helm, Paul. "Calvin and Bernard on Freedom and Necessity: A Reply to Brümmer." *Religious Studies* 30 (1994) 457–65.

———. *Calvin and the Calvinists*. Carlisle, PA: Banner of Truth Trust, 1982.

———. "The Philosophical Issue of Divine Foreknowledge." In *The Grace of God, the Bondage of the Will*, edited by Thomas R. Schreiner and Bruce A. Ware, 2:485–97. Grand Rapids: Baker, 1995.

Heppe, Heinrich. *Reformed Dogmatics*. Translated by G. T. Thompson. Grand Rapids: Baker, 1956.

Hicks, John Mark. "The Theology of Grace in the Thought of Jacobus Arminius and Philip Van Limborch: A Study in the Development of Seventeenth-Century Dutch Arminianism." PhD diss., Westminster Theological Seminary, 1985.

———. "Was Arminius an Open Theist?: Meticulous Providence in the Theology of Jacob Arminius." In *Rediscovering Arminius: Beyond the Reformed and Wesleyan Divide*, edited by Keith D. Stanglin, Mark G. Bilby, and Mark H. Mann, 137–60. Nashville: Kingswood, 2014.

Hodge, Charles. *Systematic Theology*. 3 vols. Reprint, Grand Rapids: Eerdmans, 1995.

Hoekema, Anthony A. *Created in God's Image*. Grand Rapids: Eerdmans, 1988.

Hoenderdaal, Gerrit Jan. "The Debate about Arminius Outside the Netherlands." In *Leiden University in the Seventeenth Century: An Exchange of Learning*, edited by Th. H. Lunsingh Scheurleer and G. H. M. Posthumus Meyjes, 137–59. Leiden: Universitaire Pers Leiden, 1975.

———. "The Life and Struggle of Arminius in the Dutch Republic." In *Man's Faith and Freedom: The Theological Influences of Jacobus Arminius*, edited by Gerald O. McCulloh, 11–26. New York: Abingdon, 1962.

Hoitenga, Dewey J. *John Calvin and the Will*. Foreword by Richard A. Muller. Grand Rapids: Baker, 1997.

Junius, Franciscus. *A Treatise on True Theology: With the Life of Francicus Junius*. Translated by David C. Noe. Grand Rapids: Reformed Heritage, 2014.

Kawerau, Peter Gustav. "Synergism." In *The New Schaff-Herzog Encyclopedia of Religious Knowledge*, edited by Samuel Macauley Jackson. New York: Funk and Wagnalls, 1911.

Kelly, John Norman Davidson. *Early Christian Doctrines*. Rev. ed. New York: Harper Collins, 1978.

Kendall, R. T. *Calvin and English Calvinism to 1649*. London: Oxford University Press, 1979.

Bibliography

———. "The Puritan Modification of Calvin's Theology." In *John Calvin: His Influence in the Western World*, edited by W. Stanford Reid, 199–214. Grand Rapids: Zondervan, 1982.

Kirkpatrick, Frank G. "Is the Notion of Divine Basic Act a Necessary and Sufficient Way of Talking About God's Actions in the World?" *Religious Studies* 30 (1994) 181–92.

Lake, Donald M. "Jacobus Arminius' Contribution to a Theology of Grace." In *Grace Unlimited*, edited by Clark H. Pinnock, 223–42. Minneapolis: Bethany Fellowship, 1975.

Lane, A. N. S. "Did Calvin Believe in Freewill?" *Vox Evangelia* 12 (1981) 72–90.

———. *John Calvin: Student of the Church Fathers*. Grand Rapids: Baker, 1999.

Langston, Douglas Charles. "When Willing Becomes Knowing: The Voluntarist Analysis of God's Omniscience (Duns Scotus)." PhD diss., University of California Irvine, 1982.

Laytham, D. Brent. "The Place of Natural Theology in the Theological Method of John Calvin and Jacobus Arminius." In *Church Divinity*, edited by John H. Morgan, 22–44. Bristol, IN: Wyndham Hall, 1990.

Leith, John. "Calvin's Theological Method and the Ambiguity of His Theology." In *Reformation Studies: Essays in Honor of Roland H. Bainton*, 106–14. Richmond, VA: John Knox, 1962.

———. "The Doctrine of the Will in the Institutes of the Christian Religion." In *Reformatio Perennis: Essays on Calvin and the Reformation in Honor of Ford Lewis Battles*, edited by B. A. Gerrish, 49–66. Pittsburgh: Pickwick, 1981.

Luther, Martin. *The Bondage of the Will*. Translated by Henry Cole. Grand Rapids: Baker, 1976.

MacCulloch, Diarmaid. "Arminius and the Arminians." *History Today* 39 (October 1989) 27–34.

MacGregor, Kirk R. *Luis de Molina: The Life and Theology of the Founder of Middle Knowledge*. Grand Rapids: Zondervan, 2015.

McCulloh, Gerald, editor. *Man's Faith and Freedom: The Theological Influence of Jacobus Arminius*. Nashville: Abingdon, 1962.

McGrath, Gavin John. "Puritans and the Human Will: Voluntarism within Mid-Seventeenth-Century English Puritanism as Seen in the Works of Richard Baxter and John Owen (Baxter Richard, Owen John)." PhD diss., University of Durham, 1989.

McGinn, Bernard. "Introduction." In *On Grace and Free Choice*, by Bernard of Clairvaux, translated by Daniel O'Donovan, 3–50. Kalamazoo, MI: Cistercian, 1977.

McKee, Elsie Anne, and Brian G. Armstrong. *Probing the Reformed Tradition: Historical Studies in Honor of Edward A. Dowey Jr.* Louisville: John Knox, 1989.

McNeill, John T. *The History and Character of Calvinism*. London: Oxford University Press, 1977.

Molina, Luis de. *Concordia liberi arbitri cum gratiae divina praescientia, providential, praedestinatione et reprobatione*. Edited by Johann Rabeneck. Onia and Madrid: Collegium Maximum Societatis Jesu, 1953.

Muller, Richard A. "Arminius and the Reformed Tradition." *Westminster Theological Journal* 70 (2008) 19–48.

———. "Arminius and the Scholastic Tradition." *Calvin Theological Journal* 24 (1989) 263–77.

———. "The Christological Problem in the Thought of Jacobus Arminius." *Nederlands Archief voor Kerkgeschiedenis* 68 (1988) 145–63.

Bibliography

———. *Dictionary of Latin and Greek Theological Terms: Drawn Principally from Protestant Scholastic Theology*. Grand Rapids: Baker, 1985.

———. "The Federal Motif in Seventeenth Century Arminian Theology." *Nederlands Archief voor Kerkgeschiedenis* 62/1 (1982) 102–22.

———. "*Fides* and *Cognitio* in Relation to the Problem of Intellect and Will in the Theology of John Calvin." *Calvin Theological Journal* 25 (1990) 207–24.

———. "Forward." In *John Calvin and the Will*, by Dewey J. Hoitenga, 5–11. Grand Rapids: Baker, 1997.

———. *God, Creation, and Providence in the Thought of Jacob Arminius*. Grand Rapids: Baker, 1991.

———. "God, Predestination, and the Integrity of the Created Order: A Note on Patterns in Arminius' Theology." In *Later Calvinism: International Perspectives*, edited by W. Fred Graham, 431–46. Kirksville, MO: Sixteenth Century Journal, 1994.

———. "Grace, Election, and Contingent Choice: Arminius's Gambit and the Reformed Response." In *The Grace of God, the Bondage of the Will*, edited by Thomas R. Schreiner and Bruce A. Ware, 251–78. Grand Rapids: Baker, 1995.

———. "The Priority of the Intellect in the Soteriology of Jacob Arminius." *Westminster Theological Journal* 55 (1993) 55–72.

———. "Scholasticism in Calvin: A Question of Relation and Disjunction." In *Calvinus Sincerioris Religionis Vindex*, edited by Wilhelm Neuser and Brian Armstrong, 247–65. Kirksville, MO: Sixteenth Century Journal, 1997.

———. *The Unaccommodated Calvin: Studies in the Foundation of a Theological Tradition*. New York: Oxford University Press, 2000.

Muller, Richard A., and Keith Stanglin. "*Bibliographia Arminiana*: A Comprehensive, Annotated Bibliography of the Works of Arminius." In *Arminius, Arminianism, and Europe: Jacobus Arminius (1559/60–1609)*, edited by Theodoor Marius Van Leeuwen, Keith D. Stanglin, and Marijke Tolsma, 263–90. Leiden: Brill, 2009.

Musculus, Wolfgangus. *Common Places of Christian Religion*. London, 1563.

Nicholas, James. *Calvinism & Arminianism Compared in Their Principles and Tendency*. London: Longman, 1824.

Niesel, Wilhelm. *The Theology of Calvin*. Translated by Harold Knight. Great Britain: Lutterworth, 1956.

Olson, Roger E. *Arminian Theology: Myths and Realities*. Downers Grove, IL: InterVarsity, 2006.

Packer, James I. "Luther against Erasmus." *Concordia Theological Monthly* 37/4 (1966) 207–21.

Partee, Charles. "Calvin and Determinism." *Christian Scholar's Review* 5/2 (1975) 123–29.

Pask, Alfred H. "The Influence of Arminius on John Wesley." *London Quarterly and Holborn Review* 185 (October 1960) 258–63.

Pinnock, Clark H. "From Augustine to Arminius: A Pilgrimage in Theology." In *The Grace of God, the Will of Man: A Case for Arminianism*, edited by Clark H. Pinnock, 15–30. Grand Rapids: Zondervan, 1989.

Praamsma, Louis. "The Background of the Arminian Controversy (1586–1618)." In *Crisis in the Reformed Churches*, edited by Peter Y. De Jong, 22–38. Grand Rapids: Reformed Fellowship, 1968.

Rahner, Karl and Herbert Vorgrimler. *Dictionary of Theology*. 2nd ed. New York: Crossroad, 1981.

Bibliography

Rattenbury, H. Morley. "The Historical Background and Life of Arminius." *London Quarterly and Holborn Review* 185 (October 1960) 242–48.

Reichenbach, Bruce R. "Freedom, Justice, and Moral Responsibility." In *The Grace of God, the Will of Man: A Case for Arminianism*, edited by Clark H. Pinnock, 277–303. Grand Rapids: Zondervan, 1989.

Sell, Alan P. F. *The Great Debate: Calvinism, Arminianism and Salvation*. United Kingdom: H. E. Walter, 1982. Reprint, Eugene, OR: Wipf & Stock, 1998.

Schaff, Philip, editor. *The Creeds of Christendom*. 3 vols. Revised by David S. Schaff. 6th ed. Grand Rapids: Baker, 1996.

Schreiner, Susan Elizabeth. *The Theater of His Glory: Nature and the Natural Order in the Thought of John Calvin*. Durham, NC: Labyrinth, 1991.

Schulze, L. F. "Calvin's Defense of the Will in Bondage according to the *Institutes* with Reference to a Few of His Contemporaries." In *John Calvin's Institutes: His Opus Magnum*, edited by A. D. Pont and J. Van der Walt, 164–73. Potchefstroom: Institute of Reformational Studies, 1986.

———. "Calvin's Reply to Pighius—A Micro and Macro View." In *Calvinus Ecclesias Genevensis Custos*, edited by Wilhelm Neuser, 171–85. Frankfurt: Peter Lang, 1984.

Sharp, Larry D. "The Doctrines of Grace in Calvin and Augustine." *Evangelical Quarterly* 52/1 (1980) 84–96.

Shaw, Mark R. "William Perkins and the New Pelagians: Another Look at the Cambridge Predestination Controversy of the 1590s." *Westminster Theological Journal* 58 (1996) 267–301.

Shedd, William G. T. *A History of Christian Doctrine*. 2 vols. 9th ed. Minneapolis: Klock & Klock, 1978.

Shepherd, Victor A. *The Nature and Function of Faith in the Theology of John Calvin*. Macon, GA: Mercer University Press, 1983.

Sproul, Robert C. *Willing to Believe: The Controversy over Freewill*. Grand Rapids: Baker, 1997.

Stanglin, Keith. "Arminius and Arminianism: An Overview of Current Research." In *Arminius, Arminianism, and Europe: Jacobus Arminius (1559/60–1609)*, edited by Theodoor Marius Van Leeuwen, Keith D. Stanglin, and Marijke Tolsma, 3–24. Leiden: Brill, 2009.

———. *Arminius on the Assurance of Salvation: The Context, Roots, and Shape of the Leiden Debate, 1603–1609*. Leiden: Brill, 2007.

———. "*Bona Conscientia Paradisus*: An Agustinian-Arminian Trope." In *Church and School in Early Modern Protestantism: Studies in Honor of Richard A. Muller on the Maturation of a Theological Tradition*, edited by Jordan J. Ballor, David S. Sytsma, and Jason Zuidema, 361–72. Leiden: Brill, 2013..

———, Mark G. Bilby, and Mark H. Mann. *Reconsidering Arminius: Beyond the Reformed and Wesleyan Divide*. Nashville: Kingswood, 2014.

Stelten, Leo F. *Dictionary of Ecclesiastical Latin*. Peabody, MA: Hendrickson, 1995.

Stuermann, Walter E. *A Critical Study of Calvin's Concept of Faith*. Ann Arbor: Edwards Brothers, 1952.

Talbot, Kenneth G., and W. Gray Crampton. *Calvinism, Hyper-Calvinism and Arminianism*. Lakeland, FL: Whitefield, 1990.

Taylor, Richard. *Encyclopedia of Philosophy*. Edited by Paul Edwards. 8 vols. New York: Macmillan, 1967.

Torrance, Thomas F. *Calvin's Doctrine of Man*. London: Lutterworth, 1957.

Bibliography

Tyacke, Nicholas. *Anti-Calvinists: The Rise of English Arminianism c. 1590–1640*. Oxford: Oxford University Press, 1987.

Ursinus, Zacharias. *The Commentary of Dr. Zacharias Ursinus on the Heidelberg Catechism*. Translated by G. W. Williard. Grand Rapids: Eerdmans, 1954.

Van Holk, Lambertus. "From Arminius to Arminianism in Dutch Theology." In *Man's Faith and Freedom: The Theological Influences of Jacobus Arminius*, edited by Gerald O. McCulloh, 27–45. New York: Abingdon, 1962.

Van Leeuwen, Theodoor Marius, Keith D. Stanglin, and Marijke Tolsma, editors. *Arminius, Arminianism, and Europe: Jacobus Arminius (1559/60–1609)*. Leiden: Brill, 2009.

Vermigli, Peter Martyr. *The Common Places*. Translated and edited by Anthonie Marten. London, 1583.

Vos, Arvin. *Aquinas, Calvin, and Contemporary Protestant Thought: A Critique of Protestant Views on the Thought of Thomas Aquinas*. Grand Rapids: Christian University Press (Eerdmans), 1985.

Wakefield, Gordon S. "Arminianism in the Seventeenth and Eighteenth Century." *London Quarterly and Holborn Review* 185 (October 1960) 253–58.

Ware, Bruce A. "The Place of Effectual Calling and Grace in a Calvinist Soteriology." In *The Grace of God, the Bondage of the Will*, edited by Thomas R. Schreiner and Bruce A. Ware, 2:339–63. Grand Rapids: Baker, 1995.

Warren, Bern M. "A Theological Compend of The Works of James Arminius." PhD diss., Northern Baptist Theological Seminary, 1954.

Wendel, Francois. *Calvin: Origins and Development of His Religious Thought*. Translated by Philip Mairet. Grand Rapids: Baker, 1997.

Winter, Ernst F., trans. *Erasmus–Luther: Discourse on Free Will*. New York: Ungar, 1961.

Witt, William Gene. "Creation, Redemption and Grace in the Theology of Jacobus Arminius." 2 vols. PhD diss., University of Notre Dame, 1993.

Wolter, Allan B., translator. *Duns Scotus on the Will and Morality*. Edited by William A. Frank. Washington, DC: Catholic University of America Press, 1997.

www.ingramcontent.com/pod-product-compliance
Lightning Source LLC
Chambersburg PA
CBHW070926160426
43193CB00011B/1593